# Life

# After Loss

## Bringing Hope to the Soul

by

### Becca Keating

Printed in the United States of America
Published by Becca Keating
ISBN-9798716934610

First Edition

Large quantities of this title may be requested from Amazon.com

Scripture taken from the NEW AMERICAN STANDARD BIBLES ®, Copyright © 1960, 1962, 1963, 1968, 1971,1972, 1973, 1975, 1977, 1995 by The Lockman Foundation. Used by permission.

Warning — Disclaimer:
The purpose of the book is to educate, encourage and inspire. The author and publisher shall have neither liability nor responsibility to anyone with respect to any loss or damage caused, or alleged to be caused, directly or indirectly by the information contain in this book.

I dedicate this book to my

beloved family and friends who have

walked with me through stages of life and loss.

I am blessed beyond measure because of my

Lord and Savior Jesus Christ who

is the Alpha and Omega!

# Acknowledgements

There are so many people who have supported and encouraged me on this journey of writing books. Thanks to all (and you know who you are) who have prayed for me, given me feedback, cheered me on, asking the Lord to bless this project and to open extraordinary opportunity for this book to minister to those who are wounded and grieving from the losses in their lives.

A big **thank you** to Janice Hunt who read through each chapter, letting me know of any grammatical errors and helping make each paragraph communicate a meaningful message of hope! She is uniquely designed to see every "jot and tittle" so that every sentence is as clear as possible. Thanks to Marilyn Tolson who offered time to make this project better yet. Her wisdom and insight was heaven sent. Thank you for challenging my thinking and my writing skills. May the Lord richly bless you for generously investing in my life and my work! God bless you!

I give thanks daily for Bill Keller who has encouraged me and supported me through the months of interviewing individuals in preparation for writing this book!! He has supported my effort of writing day after day plus listening to me read aloud each chapter to see if any of it made sense. He is truly my partner in this mission of publishing this book in hopes of encouraging others to trust our Lord and Savior, walking in His truth. I am so thankful and so blessed!

What a blessing to work with my graphic designer, Eric Dean. He has been attentive and professional as well as kind and patient. Thanks for attempting to dive into my brain to figure out my ideas and thoughts. You have learned to read my mind. Your artistic skills are extraordinary, accompanied by your Godly character which makes your work an answer to prayer. You are awesome!

And to each and every person interviewed for this book, thank you for sharing "your story" with me so that many more may see that there is life after loss. Thank you for your faithfulness to walk with the Lord even though life brings deep valleys to walk through. May your life stories bring hope to the soul to every reader of this book. Lord bless you all!!

I'm especially thankful for my pastor Jack Hibbs! His commitment to the Bible is reflected in his extraordinary shepherding which has enriched my life and walk with the Lord. I thank the Lord daily for him! **Thank you** for contributing the Introduction to this book!

Of course, I thank the Lord God for His love and graciousness as I struggled to see how He could use me to convey His message of hope to the world. His love and care towards us is unfathomable. To God be the glory!

# Contents

# Introduction

I am not certain as to the reason, but I have become much more aware of the magnitude of human suffering these days. It could be that being older and a grandparent, I'm more aware of how good things used to be compared to how they are today. Or maybe it's because, as a pastor, I hear a great deal from people going through various trials and I am aware of their pain and sorrow. Even though the church that I am a part of is a large, wonderful congregation, it is not exempt from suffering and the tragedy of human loss. Regardless, every day I find myself taking greater comfort in the power, reasoning and perspective that is found in the Bible regarding suffering.

When crises and difficult times come to our lives, we tend to gravitate toward one of two beliefs. One challenges our faith and causes us to question God; How could such a terrible thing happen to me? This train of thought is wrought with problems that only intensify the situation. When we attempt to take back the reins of our lives and leave God out, it leaves us hopeless, doubtful and wondering if God still loves us.

The opposing view is one that is rooted and grounded in the truth of God and the reality of Scripture. Nowhere in the Bible does it teach that bad people suffer bad things and good people enjoy good things. The truth is, in this fallen world all people experience both good and bad, pleasure and pain, joy and hardship.

The apostle James spoke to this, encouraging us as brothers and sisters, that it is wise to remember that when troubles come our way, we ought to consider it as an opportunity for great joy. In fact, Christians who have endured difficulty often reflect a deep and abiding rest that seems to almost emanate from them. How can this be? It is while we are in the furnace of refining that we sense His presence; in our hour of trial, God's promises come alive. Trying times produce a depth of character that, when tested, enable us to take on the next challenge.

Becca Keating brings light to the struggles we wrestle with and the unexpected trials we face. She shares with us the pathway to victory as she presents one encouraging message after another. No matter how dark or lonely a place you may find yourself, you'll discover pages filled with insights to help you embrace life's most challenging moments and see how God's Word brings illumination and hope to your life.

**Jack Hibbs, Pastor, Calvary Chapel Chino Hills**

The year 2020 was definitely a time of extraordinary challenge individually as well as nationally. The world was hit with a virus, causing fear, panic and despair. Many afraid to die, some afraid to suffer and others wondering what this virus was really all about. The lockdowns in our country protected the spread of the virus but have also caused numerous losses of various kinds. Loss is not foreign to our existence as human beings. Through the centuries we have experienced a myriad of different kinds of losses from mass annihilation to the loss of our car keys.

Not to minimize the heartbreak and pain of loss, what seems most important is our response to the losses we encounter. Some may experience deep depression. Some may experience confusion or despair. Some may become angry and bitter. Some may just be sad for a short time. So what determines one's outlook or response to loss? The Bible tells us to "…not be conformed to this world, but be transformed by the renewing of your mind so that you may prove what the will of God is, that which is good and acceptable and perfect." (Romans 12:2)

Does our response to loss have much to do with our perception of reality, seeing things from God's point of view? If so, to what narrative are we listening? What news stations are we listening to, to see what is going on in the world, in our nation, in our city? What magazines, books, internet sites and podcasts are we letting mold our thinking? And does this barrage of information help us to know the will of God, that which is good and acceptable and perfect? May we begin to see more clearly real life after our loss by letting God's word transform our thinking, and transform us!

As you read each chapter of this book, know that these losses are real with real people that have gone through what you may be going through right now. Maybe you are going through a type of loss and are stuck in "the valley of the shadow of death." May this book be an encouragement to you. May the reading of this book comfort you and draw you closer to the God of all creation who loves you beyond your wildest dreams. Be encouraged by Isaiah 40:29-31 which says, "He gives strength to the weary, and to him who lacks might He increases power. Though youths grow weary and tired, and vigorous young men stumble badly, Yet those who wait for the Lord will gain new strength; They will mount up with wings like eagles, They will run and not get tired, They will walk and not become weary."

*"As the world around us continues to embrace evil, the need for hope radically increases. God's Word holds the solution to this need: Jesus Christ's return! This is the great **hope** and promise we can hold on to in these dark days."*

*Jack Hibbs*

# Chapter

# 1

# Hope is Coming

*"Therefore, prepare your minds for action,
keep sober in spirit, fix your **hope** completely
on the grace to be brought to you at
the revelation of Jesus Christ."*

*1 Peter 1:13*

Loss is nothing new to the human race but is mostly met with anguish and despair. If it is so common, why are we thrown into an emotional whirlwind whenever it occurs? Is it because of our human tendencies to desire comfort and consistency? Is it that we distain change? Some people may feel out of control when loss occurs. Even losing the keys to our car can be so frustrating and humiliating. Jesus talked about loss: loss of a coin, loss of a lamb, loss of a son. When He talked about it there was always a lesson to be learned. So what can we learn from these times of loss in our lives?

Jesus said, "Do not let your heart be troubled; believe in God, believe also in Me." (John 14:1) He was explaining to His disciples that He would be leaving this earth. He was letting them know ahead of time of the loss that would be coming soon. Would that help us to know about future loss? Maybe! For me, I knew my marriage was coming to an end in 1996. I hoped and prayed that the love we had would never fade. This loss turned out to be one of the most difficult in my life, something I never wanted or dreamed would occur. The Lord gave grace and mercy. He always does when we rest in Him. The Lord is faithful to walk with us through those difficult times even though it is painful.

In 1998, I lost my father. He went home to be with the Lord after some health issues. We were aware that his days were numbered. We knew where he was going when he died, but it was still a loss and a very sad one at that. He was one of the most godly men I had ever known. My dad exemplified Jesus. His kindness and patience were always visible. He loved the Lord and God's Word. It was through the Bible teaching of my father that I came to Christ as a young teenager.

In 2000, I lost my only brother to oral cancer. It was mostly sad for my mother since one never thinks your son or daughter will pass away before you. My mother knew that his passing would mean he was no longer in pain, and sometimes knowing that helps us deal with our losses. To honor him at his memorial, he was given a military gun salute which always makes a mother proud during a time of loss.

When I moved to California from Arizona in 2004 I left many friends behind. People thought I was crazy to leave an area where I had grown up and lived for over 50 years. By this time, all of my daughters were now in California, so I stepped out in faith and made the move. There was a feeling of loss but also a gain of being closer to my children and future grandchildren. In the meantime, I returned once a month to Arizona where I would visit and tend to the affairs of my mother.

My mom had amazing faith and love for the word of God. She would sometimes forget where her glasses or keys were but she never forgot all the verses she memorized from the Bible. She stayed strong until she went home to be with the Lord in 2007. Although this loss was anticipated because of her age, I still think of her every day and often want to pick up the phone to call her, but she's in heaven and I don't have that direct number. :-) Just knowing that my father and mother are home with the Lord brings great comfort.

Back in California, my life continued to be busy: running a home-based wellness business, overseeing property purchased in Scottsdale, AZ., singing in the choir at church and learning in-depth theology from the two seminary students who rented rooms in my house. Life was full. Life was interesting as I continued to build friendships and become more involved in the community in which I lived. As time passed, life became *so* busy that juggling it all often became overwhelming. The economy and housing market was shifting. I originally thought of living in my home for a short time and then selling it for a profit, however that option was no longer obtainable. Properties were upside down. So I began improving my California home hoping to add to the value of this property or at least to maintain its value. The property in Scottsdale was also losing value. The rent I had been collecting on that house plummeted to the point of having a major deficit each month.

By 2012, I was losing my Scottsdale house and by year's end lost my California home. Without explaining all the details, losing two homes in one year was never on my "to-do list". Now I was homeless?? I never saw that coming! Lord, now what do you want me to do? What plan do you have in this loss? He would give me that answer after returning from managing two Congressional campaigns, one in California and one in Arizona.

While at church one Sunday listening to a sermon on the Proverbs of the Bible, the Lord whispered to me in that still small voice: "Becca, I want you to write a book on communication. I want you to write about the things I've taught you from My Word about communicating, about how we should listen and talk to each other." Can you imagine my reply? "What!! But Lord, I don't know how to write a book. I wouldn't know the first thing about writing a book! You can't be serious, Lord!"

After that conversation with the Lord, I finally said, "Ok, ok, ok, I will walk in faith. I will take steps to write this book you want me to write. But You are going to help me, right?" Shortly after this, one of my daughters introduced me to a man who had recently written a book. Over coffee, he walked me through the details of writing and publishing. So step by step I started this journey of writing a book. A friend from choir mentioned he had gotten laid off from the Jet Propulsion Lab in Pasadena where he edited scientific literature. He then offered to edit my book. Whoa!! Thank you, Jesus! As it turns out, another friend of my daughter who was an actress in the "industry" offered to do a photo shoot for my book showing different facial expressions and body language. She was a sister in the Lord as well as a lot of fun and a total blessing. The editor from choir also was an amazing photographer. He offered to do a photo shoot of me on location at the ranch  where I was now living. As it turned out, he took one of the photos and designed the cover of the book. From start to finish, The Secrets of Powerful Communication was written and published in six months. The Lord was definitely in on this!

So there *is* life after loss! If someone had told me ten years ago that I would be writing books and traveling across this nation speaking, I would not have believed them. But here I am, by God's grace, writing my sixth book and humbled by this whole adventure. God is so good! He has never left me nor forsaken me. He has supplied all my needs according to His riches in Christ Jesus.
(Philippians 4:19)

At the time the Lord gave me the idea to write *this* book, I interviewed a couple of people but then put this idea aside. In 2020, the Lord let me know, "OK! Write *this* book **now**!" So many people were experiencing a variety of losses and seemed overcome by fear. Some lost their businesses. Some lost the community of support from church. Some committed suicide. Some lost being with friends at school. Some lost opportunity to be with their sports team. Some lost loved ones because of a virus. So many losses! Thus the writing of this book came about in order to encourage all those who have gone through any painful time in the past and possibly more in the future. May you be assured that we have a loving and compassionate God who walks with us each day, even though we walk through the dark valleys of life. We can fix our hope completely on the grace to be brought to us in Christ Jesus.

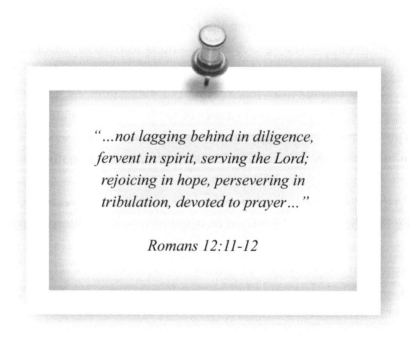

*"...not lagging behind in diligence, fervent in spirit, serving the Lord; rejoicing in hope, persevering in tribulation, devoted to prayer..."*

*Romans 12:11-12*

# Chapter

# 2

# Olivia means Peace

---

*"Peace I leave with you; My peace I give to you;*
*not as the world gives do I give to you.*
*Do not let your heart be troubled,*
*nor let it be fearful."*

*John 14:27*

I first met Becca Kopas at her 4th birthday party when her family came to visit Arizona from Baton Rouge, Louisiana, where she was born. All that time I thought her parents named her after me since I had known them since college. Turns out I think they just liked the name Rebecca. Truth be known, her parents assured me they did love that name and they believed there was a wonderful connection with me. Even so, I took pride in hearing about this spunky young child as she grew. I was always amazed how her love for the Lord shone through her life even in high school and into college. When she decided to go to medical school I was not surprised as she was very smart and motivated. As it turned out, Med school was where she met her future husband, Brice. At the wedding of Becca and Brice their love for God and their desire to glorify Him in their marriage left me wondering how these two doctors would make life work. Oh me of little faith!

Because of the foundation of their faith and their study of God's Word, I should have known the Lord was preparing them for great things. As time passed they were blessed with three children. Becca became the "main mamma" leaving Brice to balance his pediatric practice. Their life was full and busy as most young families tend to be, making time for extended family, fellowshipping with the Body of Christ and home-schooling the children. Their house and expanding back yard became a favorite place for friends to gather. Exchanging time with their close friends for a Bar-B-Q and swim party was always a success, especially during those hot summer months in Arizona.

During one of those afternoons of fellowship, the laughter and activity of the children around the pool was festive and heartwarming. That is, until it was brought to their attention that the youngest daughter, Olivia, was at their side one moment...and in less than five minutes was at the bottom of the jacuzzi. As doctors, Becca and Brice knew how to resuscitate a drowned victim. With paramedics on the way, Brice did all he could to bring life to this sweet child. When the paramedics arrived their only hope was to rush Olivia to the hospital to give her extra emergency care. As Becca and Brice followed the ambulance to the nearby hospital, they determined never to blame one another for anything. Being in the medical field, they knew that Olivia's chance of survival was very slim. They knew that whatever happened was from the hand of a good and loving God, for their best, even though their emotions felt otherwise. As much as they would wonder what they could have done differently, they knew they could not add a single minute or day to Olivia's life.

Olivia was two years and nineteen days when she went home to be with the Lord that horrific and unsettling day. Becca's mom remembers Brice and Becca coming home from the hospital after having said goodbye to Olivia for the last time. Becca's eyes were deep pools of grief, sadness, loss and everything one might think she would be feeling at that time. It was indescribable. As the memorial was being planned, Becca's comfort was on the couch in her dad's arms. For days, their friends came and went, ministering in ways only deep friendship offers. The body of Christ came around them, feeding the family, encouraging them, listening and being quiet with them. To Becca and Brice and their grieving family, no words could describe what Christ's people meant at that time. God promises that because of our eternal hope in Jesus, we DO NOT grieve as the world does. Part of that promise has to do with the faithfulness of the body of believers as well. He is truly all we need!

At Olivia's memorial, Brice was able to share with the hundreds of people in the congregation that Olivia was in heaven, safe in the arms of Jesus. He shared with the audience that they, too, could go to heaven by receiving Christ as their Savior. (John 1:12-13; 3:16-17) In a later interview, Brice mentioned how Olivia's death gave opportunities to share the Gospel far and beyond what he could have even imagined. As parents, they had always taught their children about heaven and how Jesus has prepared a place for them. Even now, Olivia's sisters, brothers and cousins can't wait to be in heaven with Olivia and to be with Jesus for eternity. Olivia is an oft-mentioned person and so all of the family, including those siblings and cousins born after she went to glory, can hardly wait to see her again in heaven!

As I listened to Becca and Brice tell their story, the deep and abiding love for the Word of God was so evident. As they reflected on God's sovereign plan and His promise to walk with them through this life, they received hope and peace. Olivia means peace, reminded Becca. They learned afresh what Jesus told his disciples in John 14:27. "Peace I leave with you, My peace I give to you; not as the world gives do I give to you. Do not let your heart be troubled, nor let it be fearful." The world seems to convey that peace is the absence of trials and suffering, but God's peace is accompanied by an untroubled and unafraid heart. Becca reiterated that the Lord promises trials. Jesus tells us in John 16:33, "These things I have spoken to you, so that in Me you may have peace. In the world you will have tribulation, but take courage; I have overcome the world." She explained that through trials the Lord builds character, making us more like Jesus each day. That didn't mean her feelings always corresponded with the truth: however; this kept her dependent on the Holy Spirit and on her knees in prayer.

One of her favorite prayers was found in the book A Diary of Private Prayer by John Baille (1889-1960) which reads as follows:

*"O Thou who indwellest in our poor and shabby human life, lifting it now and then above the dominance of animal passion and greed, allowing it to shine with the borrowed lights of love and joy and peace, and making it a mirror of the beauties of a world unseen, grant that my part in the world's life today may not be to obscure the splendor of Thy presence but rather to make it more plainly visible to the eyes of my fellow men."*

Becca shared that even though her emotions felt one way, she knew God was at work. She didn't always know what the Lord was working out, but she wanted to steward her response to this tragic situation by desiring to glorify God and not to shame Him. The challenge was applying truth regardless of her emotions on any particular day. She didn't want to get in the way of what God was doing. She felt He graciously would ask her, "Are you willing to let me use you to glorify Me in this situation?"

As time progressed, both Becca and Brice experienced a perspective shift, realizing afresh the sovereignty and goodness of God. As Psalm 139:16 states, "...And in Your book were all written the days that were ordained for me, when as yet there was

17

not one of them." They believed the Lord planned for Olivia to live with them on the earth for two years and nineteen days. Nothing they could do would change His sovereign plan. When Olivia went to heaven, their two older daughters understood this truth as well.

They saw the goodness of God by preparing them ahead of time for this loss. They learned from another older couple who had gone through a similar loss of a son. This older couple taught them well…to give thanks and know this loss came from a good and loving God. They learned that pain is not always a curse but can be a blessing. Strange as that may sound, you may know those who think of pleasure only as a blessing. When those same people encounter pain, their tendency may be to think their pain/tragedy is from an angry God. Not so! "Even though I walk through the valley of the shadow of death, I fear no evil, for You (God) are with me; Your rod and Your staff, they comfort me." (Psalm 23:4)

Though they experienced deep grief, the Holy Spirit faithfully moved and gave so many opportunities to magnify the Lord. When others learned of Olivia's death, it gave Brice multiple opportunities to preach the Gospel. In the interview, Brice mentioned how he thought Olivia was a little slow in developing her speech. He thought when she grew up God would take Olivia's weakness in speech, opening her mouth to boldly preach the Gospel. He never dreamed God would use Olivia's death to speak to the multitudes, proclaiming the good news of the Gospel. Keep in mind, Brice is a pediatrician, a doctor of many families with many children. His outreach in their community became over and above what he could have ever imagined. Even to this day, with two more children added to their quiver, Brice and Becca are having an awesome impact in their community and in their sphere of influence.

A long time later Becca confided that she once thought that if this kind of thing ever happened to her she would be a useless puddle on the floor. But God has seen her through, and today there is so much about her that has been shaped by God into a deeper character, more mature perspective and understanding of who He is and who she is in Him. The Lord's peace surely overcomes this world. As for Brice, he would say that he felt as though he had lost *everything* in losing Olivia. But today, there is that same shaping in his life as Becca has experienced in hers. They both live joyful lives as they continue to walk together with their Lord and Savior.

*"Be anxious for nothing, but in everything by prayer and supplication with thanksgiving let your requests be made known to God. And the **peace** of God which surpasses all comprehension, will guard your hearts and minds in Christ Jesus."*

*Philippians 4:6-7*

# Chapter

# 3

# JAM No More

---

*"And do not be conformed to this world,*
*but be transformed by the renewing of your mind*
*so that you may prove what the will of God is,*
*that which is good and acceptable and perfect."*

*Romans 12:2*

Remember back in the 1970s when rock and roll was at its peak? Yeah, me neither! But it definitely was a time to remember for Dennis whose strong confidence and determined spirit allowed his entertainment and events business to bring in millions each year. From 1973, his thought to be an agent booking musicians turned into booking bands which turned into booking large events for some of the most famous and prominent people in California. He started locally in Orange County with groups some may remember like: Papa Doo Run Run, Ronny and the Classics, Antix, the Hodads, Justin Tusk, Lil Elmo and the Cosmos, Splash and Surf City Allstars just to name a few. Don't you just love some of the names of those groups; so creative. Honestly, I didn't make this up.

The Associations, Bob Hope, Juice Newton, Gary Puckett and the Union Gap, Otis Day and the Knights, the Tokens, Eddie Rabbit, Janis Ian, the Drifters, the Coasters and Marveletts are names probably more familiar to many. For Dennis, they were his clients and those who often thought of him as a friend. They trusted him to produce the best events which sometimes became so large he would need to find a large open field, bringing in staging, sound crew, catering, port-a-potties and most importantly, security. Organizing a fund raising event with the House of Blues to bringing in "look alike" actors and actresses, posing as Elvis and Marilyn Monroe, was always a big hit.

There seemed to be nothing Dennis and his growing staff couldn't do but there were definitely things his company, JAM, wouldn't do...no drugs, no porn, no dirty comedians. Those who wanted JAM to organize and run the events included Dreamworks Animation, Warner Brothers, Fletcher Jones, Allergan, ESPN,

Black Angus, Biltmore Hotel, St. Regis Hotel, Balboa Bay Club, Surf and Sand Hotel and the House of Blues which kept him very busy especially in southern California. There were challenges from time to time...like the time his billionaire client wanted a baby rhinoceros as part of the "petting zoo" at his home for his son's birthday party. That didn't stop Dennis!

One major event did happen in 1977, when one sweet gal wouldn't give him what he wanted because the Bible stated a specific guideline. He was raised Catholic and thought he knew all about what the Bible had to say. He was *certain* that this thing called fornication was not in the Bible! So he drove to the closest Berean book store and bought himself a Bible. Reading his new Bible from cover to cover, he was astounded how many times this subject was mentioned. He was determined to find out more about what this Bible had to say so decided to visit a nearby Calvary Chapel church whose pastor was the memorable Chuck Smith Sr. To make a long and glorious story shorter, Dennis came to Christ. He received Jesus Christ as his personal Savior and was baptized in the ocean's Back Bay by Pastor Billy Dobrenan. A cool thing happened when Dennis came out of the water of baptism: A shaft of light beamed down through the clouds on both the pastor and himself. This was definitely a significant event in the life of Dennis.

Business was still booming. In the 80s and 90s, disc jockeys became an asset that made creating events easier and more portable. Dennis literally had hundreds of disc jockeys, some bi-lingual, covering weddings, birthday parties, anniversaries and of course every possible special event. Things were going so amazingly well that Dennis opened up a huge, two-suite office in Costa Mesa, California. Life was good. God was good. Dennis was faithful to be involved in a local church serving as head usher, attending weekly services and Bible studies. His notoriety continued to grow along with his successful business. If you wanted an extraordinary event, JAM was the company to call!

In 2007, Dennis and his wife took a cruise to relax and escape the hectic schedule. While on the ship, he felt led by the Holy Spirt to meet a man whom he had seen earlier showing authentic love toward another. As the cruise was coming to an end, Dennis was finally able to have a conversation with this man who happened to be a pastor/missionary. At the end of their conversation, the pastor looked up to the heavens and said, "Thank You, Lord!" After that, the pastor told Dennis that when he would return to work, things were **not** going to go well. He told Dennis, "the enemy wants to sift you like sand." At that point, Dennis laughed out loud knowing how successful he had been and how well things had gone for over 30 years. Dennis and new friend, Maryland, said their goodbyes but promised to stay in touch.

Dennis scoffed and laughed at the idea that "things would not go well" when he returned home. That was until he got word that his office manager, a week prior, had become very ill and would not be returning to work. Upon his return, his personal secretary resigned because she was getting married and starting a fitness business. Agents were re-examining the JAM business. One by one, Dennis was losing staff and was having to take extra time to train new staff. Discord had been occurring among the staff. By

2008, his staff was down to five people. JAM was still getting business but not the volume he was used to.

Wanting to stay in touch with his pastor friend, Maryland, talking on the phone most every day was not unusual. By 2011, Dennis took his wife to Florida to visit Maryland and his wife. It was at this time Maryland told Dennis, "You have a ministry in you and it's got to come out. JAM has to go away, then the ministry will blossom." Puzzled by this comment, Dennis began to write things that would come to his mind, things he felt the Lord was giving to him. He wasn't sure where this was heading but he knew God was guiding and directing his steps. To give him some direction, he attended a Christian conference in Washington to learn about writing and publishing.

About this same time, 2012, the economy was tanking. By 2013, he sold his office. He sold his business before there was nothing left to sell! In my interview with Dennis he reiterated that JAM had to die so that this new ministry could blossom and grow. Life after loss, indeed! In that same year, Dennis Morrison wrote and published his first book: Operation 180; the Action Plan which details the imperative of the Body of Christ to wake up in these last days! Like a boa constrictor, the world is trying to squeeze the church into its mold. Dennis details the call to action to strengthen the Body of Christ with intense study of the Bible, prayer, fasting and a trust in the Lord that wipes out all fear! Preparing the Body for these last days Dennis likens it to facing a Goliath, requiring boldness to confront and slay.

In 2015, the Lord led him to write his second book: <u>Last Days Ultimate Christian Prepper</u> which explains the importance of being prepared physically and spiritually in these last days as we approach trying times! He discusses salvation, the rapture, the importance of prayer and fasting, and the importance of the Holy Spirit working in and through the lives of the believer.

Since the loss of his entertainment business God is touching lives through his writing of books as well as daily emails to nearly 100 men, plus writing articles for a conservative online news outlet. His next book will be out, Lord willing, in 2022. When talking with Dennis in our interview he stated that he is now helping people spiritually for eternity, not just entertaining them. His commitment to reading and studying the Bible each day has produced much fruit. He has become a prayer warrior for our community, our state and our nation, claiming 2 Chronicles 7:14: "And My people who are called by My name humble themselves and pray and seek My face and turn from their wicked ways, then I will hear from heaven, will forgive their sin and will heal their land." Praying for revival has become a top priority for Dennis.

When I asked him, "How are you surviving without a company bringing in millions each year?" Dennis assured me that God was supplying all of his needs according to His riches in glory in Christ Jesus. (Philippians 4:19) He knows money does not buy happiness. He also realized if he had JAM in 2020, when entertainment came to a screeching halt, he would have lost everything to a greater degree. God was gracious to bring an end to JAM before the enormous economic losses which occurred during that horrendous year. Dennis told me he has been in the company of great people like Bob Hope, but now he is serving the Great One, the God of all creation, the Lord Jesus Christ!

To learn more go to: www.DennisDmorrison.com

*"Do not let your heart be troubled; believe in God, believe also in Me... Jesus said to him, I am the way, the truth and the life; no one comes to the Father but through Me."*

*John 14:1, 6*

# Chapter

# 4

# Jackie's Story

---

*"Behold, the eye of the Lord is on those who fear Him,*
*On those who* **hope** *for His lovingkindness,*
*To deliver their soul from death…Our soul waits*
*for the Lord; He is our help and our shield."*

*Psalm 33:18-20*

Jackie and I met at an unconventional place at an unusual time in my journey of writing this book. When I mentioned to her the subject matter of this book, she began to share her story with me… and this is how it unfolded:

Jackie explained that… "Noel was a new friend but it felt like I had known her forever. We both lived in a community that felt safe and secure, so meeting her through other friends at a local church was warmly welcomed. I first met her at Calvary Westlake in the kids ministry. After exchanging hellos, I thought she looked familiar. Within the next week I saw her again in a small group Bible study that I had been attending for awhile. I was just beginning to know the ladies in the group. We laughed, told about our week's adventures and dug deeper into the word of God, going through the book of Esther. It was a great study!

As time passed, Noel and another girlfriend asked me if I was doing anything for my birthday. I said no, considering I was just going to be working that day. So she asked if I was available later on Friday because they wanted to take me out for my birthday. I thought that was so sweet so I said yes! Noel told me to dress cute!

A few days later they came to pick me up, both handing me a birthday gift as I got in the car. I was already taken back by their kindness toward me since only knowing them for a short time. We then drove to Malibu. One of the girls was practicing her photographic skills by taking photos of us on the beach. Noel was telling me the right way to look at the camera. Who knew! After that we went to a cute cafe and had lunch. These girls had been so nice to me, I thought, what can I do for them? I asked if they wanted to go hear some live music at a coffee shop. I had some friends that were playing that night so they agreed to go since we were already dressed up "so cute." Can't waste a cute outfit, right? They enjoyed the music. Later we all kept in contact and saw each other at Bible study. I was so thankful to have those friends.

Time passed. I had gone to visit my sister at college in Arizona. As I was getting back into town, I checked Noel's Snapchat where she had posted a dance floor of a bar and grill, saying "it's quiet tonight." I thought "ok" she's at Borderline. So before going to bed I was on my computer and saw an article about a shooting at a country bar. I looked at the time and thought, Oh my gosh, that's right now! Then I noticed the article stating it was Borderline.

I quickly grabbed my phone to text Noel who usually would get back to me right away. I texted, "are you ok, Borderline??" No response! I quickly got dressed, grabbed my keys and drove to Borderline. On the freeway tears started rolling down my checks. I somehow had a feeling things were not good! I was praying and telling myself that I needed to stop thinking that the worst had happened. My dad called me asking where I was going, considering I left the house close to midnight. The shooting happened around 11:20 PM. Noel's Snapchat showed the picture of the dance floor before all hell broke loose…meaning before the shooter came in to start the rampage.

When I got off the freeway the SWAT team was already there. I rolled down my window to ask where I could park. One of the SWAT guys directed me to a place nearby. I thanked him, and parked. There were already a lot of police there. I got out of the truck and grabbed my dog, thinking Noel would be able to see my dog before she saw me in all the chaos. She's a German Shepard. I leashed her and ran up the sidewalk toward the bar. I looked around and there were SWAT men standing in a line in the street holding their guns. I stopped for a second but no one seemed concerned about me approaching, so I kept going. I heard someone yell as I was getting closer toward the bar. A SWAT guy was saying something so I figured I better stop. He caught up with me and said, "You can't go further… there is an active shooter." I yelled, "Who's the shooter? Why aren't you in there killing him??"

I had so many emotions and adrenaline in my body I don't remember feeling my hands. I was scared! This was serious and I was yelling at the Swat guy…oh gosh! I told him I have a good friend in there! He looked at me and told me to get back and sit on the curb. So I found a spot and sat. Then he told me I had to go sit at the gas station across the street, so my dog and I went over there to sit and watch all the firetrucks and ambulances show up. I was praying out loud, "Dear God, please let her be alive, please God let this not be so bad, dear Jesus please keep us all safe!"

As time passed, more people gathered while I was just waiting for Noel to come down the hill. I crossed the street to where more people had gathered. I saw some people with cameras show up. I saw the FBI. My mom called me saying she was watching the news and was seeing everything gong on. I told her, "I'm not leaving yet. I haven't found Noel." Amongst all the traffic of emergency vehicles, I saw some people being allowed to walk toward the ambulances, so I went in hopes of seeing Noel. I was standing, looking and thinking to myself, "Ok, she will be down soon." I saw people with bloody arms and legs crying, hugging each other. Blankets were being put on them. Still no sight of Noel! As more people walked down, I saw my friend Bobby. He survived but was totally in shock. He had been working the bar that night and hid in the attic until help arrived. I'm so thankful he survived! I gave him a hug before he headed home.

I still waited. I watched a guy taking photos (probably for the newspaper). I was just staring, stunned. In the meantime, I received a few texts from two family friends asking if I was ok and if I was safe. I let them know I was safe but was just looking, waiting for a friend.

I started getting a sick feeling in my stomach. I kept telling myself to stay positive, especially around these people that had a near death experience. I couldn't believe this was happening. The FBI was asking if anyone had any information on the incident. I came forward to show the FBI lady Noel's Snapchat which was taken prior to the shooter going into the bar. The FBI lady took a picture of it. I asked if there was any way of knowing if my friend was still inside the bar, or if an ambulance had possibly taken her to the hospital. She didn't know but took down my phone number to notify me if Noel was located. I never did get a call.

I knew there was nothing I could do. As I headed back to my car, I noticed the media had parked and blocked my way out. There were hundreds of cameras lined up in the street, and media people were already on air live. I talked to some media people to explain how I was looking for my friend, but as yet couldn't find her. I then went to the hospital hoping Noel would already be there. I was greeted by a police officer at the emergency door who said other people were looking for her, too. In the waiting room I saw the pastors from church. We sat and talked a bit. They said there was no sign of Noel at the hospital. I told one of the pastors that I could go by her house to see if she was home. They thought that was a good idea so I headed to Noel's home.

I made it to her house at about 3:00 in the morning. Her car wasn't there. More bad feelings emerged. I knocked on the door hoping for the best. Her dad answered the door. I said, "Hi, I'm so sorry but there has been a shooting at Borderline. Noel was there but we can't find her so, I came here hoping that she would be home." I felt so bad. He did not know about the shooting at Borderline. I said "sorry" again! I felt so bad but at least now Noel's parents knew and could be praying and getting answers as well. I drove back toward Borderline thinking maybe the police would know or have more information by now.

It was suggested to me to go to the community center, so I drove there not knowing what to expect. More cops were there so I gave one of them Noel's name, letting them know I could help identify her. At this point all things were telling me she could possibly be one of the victims. I just prayed it wasn't so. I waited and waited as more people began showing up at the community center. I assumed those coming were friends and family members of the victims. The pastor from Godspeak Calvary Chapel, Rob McCoy, showed up to comfort the people. There was no luck finding her there so I left and went home.

I was still in shock. I don't think I got any sleep that night. Some friends from church came over early in the morning. The news was on the television when they announced the victims one by one. Sure enough, Noel's name came up! We all broke down in tears, hugging each other and praying. Later, some news reporters and journalists contacted me and another friend to obtain photos of Noel. In my head I was thinking, "Was this really happening?" Photos I had given them were now being broadcasted on the news. I was thinking this could have been me, too, if I had met her there last night. I couldn't believe all this madness. Things were happening so quickly, yet in slow motion at the same time, as if time was standing still.

I had people around me, good praying people. When I was with a younger group we talked and shared memories of Noel, thinking "How is this real?" We met the media at the park to talk about Noel. We traveled together to her funeral service. Seeing her body in the casket was surreal. Her mom was wailing in sorrow! I was in total shock and disbelief, realizing Noel and I were talking only a few short days ago. How could this happen? There was another service for her at Calvary Church. It was good news hearing that she was at peace and in heaven but I still had that feeling of sorrow.

To this day, I still have good memories of Noel. We were just starting to get to know each other. She had come and gone in my life so fast. We had moments of laughter and fun. She and I had a lot in common and she was so peaceful and happy the last time we hung out together. God gave me a gift of peace. There are still days when I cry and just let the tears flow. Noel was only 21 years old.

We had just celebrated her birthday with a lot of her other friends as well. It was a great time! I was thankful to be included. Good people are hard to come by these days and she was a good one!

Even now I pray a lot, thanking God for my life and the people that I still have here with me. Life gets so busy, I lose track of time. I am confident in the fact that I will be united with Noel again in heaven along with other loved ones that I have lost here on earth. Life is precious and it's best to appreciate what we have here and now. Our lives can change in an instant.

I am thankful that I have been a part of Bible studies and living in a wonderful community. Not everyone gets that opportunity and I feel truly blessed. God is so good! He is for us even in times of sorrow and loss. God is our refuge and our strength. The Lord is our help in time of trouble. He is always looking out for us and is protecting us as well. Our obedience to Him is also our safe guard. I've been raised in the church and I try to read my Bible daily, for it is the bread of life. The Bible has so many life lessons that we can relate to in the present. Jesus Christ is not only my hope, but the hope for others as well. I trust things will get better and the pain that we are going through now won't compare to our future joy that will be for us in heaven! In every trial there is always hope. In every despair there is always hope. For our God is a good God and for that I am truly thankful!"

*In memory of*
*Noel Colette Sparks*

*"But as for me,*
*I will hope continually,*
*And will praise You yet more*
*and more."*

*Psalm 71:14*

# Chapter

# 5

# Vote for Rob

---

*"Do you not know that those who run in a race*
*all run, but only one receives the prize?*
*Run in such a way that you may win!"*

*1 Corinthians 9:14*

The American Renewal Project was where I first met Rob McCoy. He was always there. Every time I had the privilege of attending these spiritually packed meetings, Rob was there working the room, encouraging others in ministry, speaking about his convictions of being involved as a conservative citizen in this great nation. I didn't realize for a long time that he was a pastor of a church in the Los Angeles area. His story was inspiring as he expounded on his journey of getting marching orders from the Lord to put feet to his faith. He was determined to do as God led.

In a recent interview with Rob, I found out so much more about him and who he has become. He had grown up in California. His dad grew up in California, and became a Naval officer on Coronado Island. His mother was involved in the Republican Women's clubs in San Diego. He remembers meeting Ronald Reagan at age ten, not realizing he was meeting a future President. His whole heritage exemplified conservative values. He registered to vote as a Republican as soon as he turned 18. Why do I bring this to your attention? Because, like Aristotle, Rob believed even at a young age that politics was the highest form of community. It combined morality with sociability. Upon that premise, Rob was keenly aware of the importance of being an active citizen, standing up for the values on which he was raised.

While in college, Rob came to Christ, taking Jesus as his personal Savior. He now had even more reasons to stand up for biblical values in the public square. As an adult, while on a tour to Israel with some well known people in the political arena, Rob conducted talks on the biblical perspective of the locations they visited. One woman on the tour, a California State Assembly member, was so impressed with Rob that she felt led to encourage him (by the prompting of the Holy Spirit) to run for political office in California. He wondered why the Holy Spirit didn't talk to him first but committed to pray with his wife about the option of running for a political office. After returning to California, the Lord gave him a couple of verses to ponder. "Though He slay me, I will hope in Him." (Job 13:15) That seemed like an odd verse but Rob grabbed on to that message from the Lord along with a verse in 1 Corinthians (9:14) "…to run in such a way that you may win."

Stepping out in faith in 2014, Rob began the process of filing papers and doing all that was required to run for California State Assembly in the district where he lived and pastored a church. His church was a growing church and had been for many years. Not only did his congregation "step up to the plate" in full support of his run but over 650 volunteers rallied around him to carry him to victory. It became the largest grass-roots effort in the past 20 years in California. What was not anticipated was the lack of support from the local churches. When Rob asked if he could visit a church so that congregants and the pastor could pray for him, he was denied. Didn't these folks want a representative with biblical, conservative values legislating for life, liberty and the pursuit of happiness? Didn't they realize he could be a missionary in the halls of government?

The political race raged on as Rob battled to get through the primary. He faced an unexpected blow from his own party who threw in a million dollars to another Republican candidate. Unbelievable! Rob had been a Republican longer than he had been married and longer than he had been a Christian. And this is what happens? Yes, you've heard it and it seems true: Politics is messy…and often vicious. But "greater is He who is in me than he who is in the world." Rob didn't back down, running his race to win…and in the primary, he did.

Now came the major uphill climb, facing off with the opposing team. With the army of volunteers and Rob's conviction to run to win, every day was filled to the brim with fund raising, walking precincts, phone calling and, of course, dealing with the media. Fund raising had gone very well despite the consultants who tried to drain the coffer. As time drew closer to election day Rob was sure of a win. Finally the day of victory came only to find out that of 100,000 votes cast, Rob lost by only 4,000 votes. Needless to say, he was devastated!! By 3:00 AM Rob messaged to his opponent his concession.

Feeling exhausted and terribly discouraged Rob lamented, "Lord, I feel like I've led these folks on a rosy road to nowhere." What was most discouraging was the lack of participation from those in the Christian community. There are more Christians in California than any other state in the union except for Texas. Sadly, only half of those are registered to vote and half of those registered don't show up unless it's the year of a presidential election. What's up with that!! As Rob grumbled to the Lord, God spoke in His still quiet voice, "Remember the verses I gave you?" (Though He slay me, I will hope in Him.) Rob affirmed yet said, "but I didn't think I would lose…and I ran to win!!" The Lord replied, "Yes, you did run to win! But I have other things in store for you."

As time passed and wounds began to heal, the folks of Thousand Oaks started encouraging Rob to run again...but for City Council. The troops rallied and the race was on for this new position. A dear friend who had recently had a stroke told Rob, "If God heals me of this speech defect, I will do phone calling for your campaign." As it turned out, this dear man was able to accomplish over 30,000 phone calls. Another dear brother took over the task of walking precincts so that Rob could continue to spend time meeting people and raising funds. The volunteer base was huge. Rob was humbled and encouraged even though it was another tough run against some very well qualified individuals.

Election day came but the numbers did NOT look good. Rob braced himself for another defeat until his buddy, Tom Hunt, assured him of a win. "How are you so sure I will win?" questioned Rob. "Of the 1200 calls I made in the last 24 hours," answered Tom, "almost every one of them are voting for you, Rob!" When the final tally came in, Rob was thrilled to hear that he had 52 votes more than the opponent. And what does it mean when a candidate wins by 52 votes? Exactly! It meant Rob was the winner!

Rob McCoy served on the Thousand Oaks City Council not just one term but two terms. He relayed to me that being in that position made him a better pastor as he *ministered* to the whole community. Then on November 8, 2018, in his second term of office when he was Mayor Pro Tem, the Borderline shooting tragically occurred killing 12 young people inside this country western bar and grill. The chaos at the scene of the massacre was horrific! In the early morning hours, Rob, along with other city council members, began hearing of the fatalities, comforting those families and friends whose loved ones were killed or injured. Can you imagine the value of having a pastor, like Rob, being available to those families in need?

It was a heart-wrenching time for the whole community, not only because of the devastating murders but because of the raging fires that swarmed through the canyons and hillsides, swallowing up home after home. Grief was rampant! As memorials were scheduled, Rob was asked to conduct two of them. The two memorials happened to be victims that were members of his own church. He and all of the council members attended each and every memorial of those shot in the Borderline massacre. The people of this community really pulled together, a sight I've seen over and over again across this great nation.

One unique event which arose from this community pulling together was a determination to erect a memorial garden. This garden would give homage to all who were killed in the Borderline massacre. With the cooperation of the City Parks and Recreation giving land and the Thousand Oaks City Council providing the funds, this memorial park was constructed and dedicated in only one year from the anniversary of the shooting, November 8, 2019. Amazing! Of course, Rob was there to help dedicate this new and beautiful Memorial Park.

Entering 2020, Rob's life was returning to its normal rhythm of pastoring his church and working on the city council...that is, until a virus and those in authority struck fear into the public and began shutting down normal life as we had known it. The governor of

California announced a lockdown, causing most businesses to close except for liquor stores, marijuana dispensaries, strip joints, and big box stores like Costco. Churches were declared NON-essential and must stay closed until the governor said otherwise. Hmmmm! That did not make much sense to Rob, who watched the unmasked rioters in downtown LA cause havoc, burning down businesses mostly owned by Jewish citizens. He knew that the Church was necessary and essential to minister to his community.

During Holy week he purposed to obey the sanitation requirements while allowing his congregation to come to the church to receive communion. People lined up to participate in this very unprecedented event. Distancing, masking, and sanitizing between each shift caused this normally brief ceremony to be over three hours in duration. Because of the decision to provide communion for his congregation, Rob was hammered by the press and social media. Within a day Rob knew he would be censored and would need to step down from the city council. Late Saturday night Rob made the call. He resigned.

Freed up to pastor his flock, Rob preached in the parking lot that next day, plus continuing to broadcast online as well as producing video clips on important topics. Reaching people with the good news from the Bible seemed the most loving thing to do, offering comfort and encouragement to his congregation and beyond. But that wasn't the sentiment of those in Sacramento. Criticism was unleashed upon Rob even though his shepherd's heart stayed compassionate and determined to not forsake the assembling of his people. His frustration was aroused, realizing that, **"Watching**

**church online was like watching a fireplace online. You can see it and hear it but you can't feel the warmth!"**

By May 31, 2020, Pentecost Sunday, Rob decided to open the church, opening wide to anyone and everyone who wanted to worship and sing praises to the Lord. Yes, sanitation measures were taken. If you wanted to wear a mask, it was up to your own discernment. Rob sought the Lord for guidance in this decision and knew that he must obey God over man, realizing the tyrannical measures that had been placed on a most essential institution is protected by the United States Constitution.

By this time, statistics were coming in regarding this virus. It was the first time in history that the public was quarantined, told to sequester at home, because of a virus. Turned out some people had the virus and didn't even know it until they were tested. Not only were stats coming in regarding the virus but other information began to surface. Business owners were losing their life investments. Overdoses and suicides were the highest for a one year period in the history of our nation. Child abuse was up 300%. The elderly were dying alone in the hospital or nursing homes because family was not allowed to advocate or be with their loved one in that situation. SO Wrong! School children had no where to go because all sports, entertainment, skate parks, etc. were shut down. Rob knew that God made people a trichotomy: body, soul and spirit. He knew the church was essential. It was **very** essential!

By late August of 2020, three of five County Supervisors in Rob's domain took action to secure an attorney (with taxpayer's money) to request a judge to put an injunction against Rob and his congregation. It was apparent that these elected supervisors had a disdain for a local body of believers who wanted to continue to freely gather and worship together. The attorney sought to have people arrested and have the church closed down by putting an emergency temporary restraining order on them, even though there had not been one single case of the virus up to that point. Rob plus 1,000 congregants or visitors would be given a citation each week of the violation of the order. Then the attorney sought to have the judge enforce the orders by pressuring sheriffs to arrest people if necessary and chain the doors of the church.

After learning of all these tyrannical orders and injunction towards Rob and the church, people were brought to their knees praying to the Lord for wisdom and protection, remembering Jeremiah 32:17, "Ah Lord God! Behold, You have made the heavens and the earth by Your great power and by Your outstretched arm! Nothing is too difficult for You." Sunday morning Rob didn't know what to expect but went to the church ready to preach and minister to his flock. What he didn't anticipate were hundreds of freedom-loving citizens from all across California and the nation, Christians and atheists alike, surrounding the church. When Rob asked, "Why are you all here?" They responded, "We have come to take the citations or be arrested so that you and your congregation can gather and worship in peace." These people showed up to protect our God-given rights secured by our Constitution. Rob's favorite poster held by a protestor stated, "It took a #!*<# governor to get this atheist to church!!" All those who came realized that if we don't defend our freedom, we will lose it!

To this day Rob continues to walk in the power of God's Word claiming, "No weapon that is formed against you will prosper; and every tongue that accuses you in judgment you will condemn. This is the heritage of the servants of the Lord, and their vindication is from Me, declares the Lord." (Isaiah 54:17) Rob loves his flock and the community in which he serves his church. He knows liberty is God's idea, not man's. He knows he has been called to be salt and light in his sphere of influence. He is committed to "be diligent to present himself approved to God as a workman who does not need to be ashamed, *accurately handling the word of truth.*" (2 Timothy 2:15) Rob also believes that "God has not given us a spirit of timidity (or fear), but of power and love and discipline." (2 Timothy 1:7) Therefore, Rob McCoy will persevere, standing strong in his calling, awakening the church to the truth, bringing hope to the soul to all who have ears to hear the good news which he proclaims. May God richly bless him, his family, his flock and his community!

*"We give thanks to God always for all of you, making mention of you in our prayers; constantly bearing in mind your work of faith and labor of love and steadfastness of **hope** in our Lord Jesus Christ in the presence of our God and Father."*

*1 Thessalonians 1:2-3*

# Chapter

# 6

# Joni's Dive

---

*"Therefore we do not lose heart, but though our outer man is decaying, yet our inner man is being renewed day by day. For momentary, light affection is producing for us an eternal weight of glory far beyond all comparison..."*

*2 Corinthians 4:16-17*

During my college years at the University of Arizona, I would often stop in the local Christian bookstore to browse, checking out the new books and the latest music cassette tapes. Remember those? One day I saw a poster of a young woman drawing with her mouth, creating beautiful nature scapes and other whimsical art. I was amazed that this gal could be so skilled at creating art while holding the pen between her teeth. Wanting to find out more about this young woman, I learned she had become paralyzed, confined to a wheel chair. She found it difficult to use her arms and couldn't use her hands at all. How did this happen? What was the cause of this paralysis?

I later learned that Joni had been in a diving accident which caused this total turn of events in her life. To best explain this tragic incident, she describes that day on July 30, 1967 in Chesapeake Bay as follows:

"As my body broke the surface in a dive, its cold cleanness doused my skin. In a jumble of actions and feelings, many things happened simultaneously. I felt my head strike something hard and unyielding. At the same time, clumsily and crazily, my body sprawled out of control. I heard or felt a loud electric buzzing, an unexplainable inner sensation. It was something like an electrical shock, combined with a vibration—like a heavy metal spring being suddenly and sharply uncoiled, its "sprong" perhaps muffled by the water. Yet it wasn't really a sound or even a feeling—just a sensation. I felt no pain."

"I heard the underwater sound of crunching, grinding sand. I was lying face down on the bottom. Where? How did I get here? Why are my arms tied to my chest? My thoughts screamed. Hey! I'm caught! I felt a small tidal undercurrent lift me slightly and let me settle once more on the bottom. Out of the corner of my eye, I saw light above me. Some of the confusion left. I remembered diving into the bay. Then what? Am I caught in a fishnet or something? I need to get out! I tried to kick. My feet must be tied or caught too! Panic seized me. With all my willpower and strength, I tried to break free. Nothing happened. Another tidal swell lifted and rolled. What's wrong? I hit my head. Am I unconscious? Trying to move is like trying to move in a dream. Impossible. But I'll drown! Will I wake up in time? Will someone see me? I can't be unconscious, or I wouldn't be aware of what's happening. No, I'm alive."

"I felt the pressure of holding my breath begin to build. I'd have to breathe soon. Another tidal swell gently lifted me. Fragments of faces, thoughts, and memories. What's wrong? I hit my head. Am I unconscious? Trying to move is like trying to move in a dream. Impossible. But I'll drown! Will I wake up in time? Will someone see me? I can't be unconscious, or I wouldn't be aware of what's happening. No, I'm alive. I felt the pressure of holding my breath begin to build. I'd have to breathe soon. Another tidal swell gently lifted me. Fragments of faces, thoughts, and memories spun crazily across my consciousness."

"Joni!" A somber voice echoed down some eerie corridor, almost as a summons. God? Death? I'm going to die! I don't want to die! Help me, please. "Joni!" Doesn't anyone care that I'm here? I've got to breathe! "Joni!" That voice! Muffled through the waters, it sounded far off. Now it was closer. "Joni, are you all right?" Kathy! My sister sees me. Help me, Kathy! I'm stuck! The next tidal swell was a little stronger than the rest and lifted me a bit higher. I fell back on the bottom, with broken shells, stones, and sand grating into my shoulders and face. "Joni, are you looking for shells?" No! I'm caught down here—grab me! I can't hold my breath any longer. "Did you dive in here? It's so shallow," I heard Kathy clearly now. Her shadow indicated she was now above me. I struggled inwardly against panic, but I knew I had no more air. Everything was going dark."

"I felt Kathy's arms around my shoulders, lifting. Oh, please, dear God. Don't let me die! Kathy struggled, stumbled, then lifted again. Oh, God, how much longer? Everything was black, and I felt I was falling while being lifted. Just before fainting, my head broke the water's surface. Air! Beautiful, life-giving, salt-tinged air. I choked in oxygen so quickly, I almost gagged. Gasping, I gulped in mouthfuls. "Oh, thank You, God—thank You!""

"Hey, are you okay?" Kathy asked. She called to a nearby swimmer on an inflated raft. Together they wrestled me onto it and pushed it toward shore. I heard the raft beneath me slide against the sandy beach. I tried to get up but felt pinned against the raft. Soon there was a crowd hovering above me, faces looking down in curiosity. Their stares and whispers made me feel embarrassed, uncomfortable, and even more confused. "Kathy, please make them leave." "Yes, everyone stand back! Someone call an ambulance. Move away, please. She needs air," Kathy instructed.

"As I lay there on the sand, I began to piece things together. I had hit my head diving; I must have injured something to cause this numbness. I wondered how long it would last. "Don't worry," I reassured Kathy and her boyfriend Butch —and myself. "The Lord won't let anything happen to me. I'll be all right." I heard the wail of a siren. Soon the ambulance pulled up and doors opened. In less than a minute, attendants efficiently lifted me onto a stretcher. Somehow their starched white uniforms were comforting as they carefully placed me in the back of the ambulance."

"Frustration and fear finally brought a flood of hot tears as I began to sense the seriousness of the situation. Yea, though I walk through the valley of the shadow of death, I will fear no evil; for thou art with me… I fought back the tears and tried to think of other things. Once in the hospital…Dr. Sherrill came in to examine me. He was holding my arm and pressing the pin against my limp fingers, wrist, and forearm. Why can't I feel anything? He touched the upper arm. Finally I felt a small sting in my shoulder. "Yes, I feel that. I had feeling there at the beach." Dr. Sherrill took out his pen and began to write on the clipboard. "Looks like a fracture-dislocation." "Uh-huh. I'd say at the fourth and fifth cervical level judging from her areas of feeling."

Time passed. Hours blurred into days.

"Everyday doctors came to see me. Sometimes they came in pairs and discussed my case. "She has total quadriplegia," one doctor explained to an associate, "the result of a diagonal fracture between the fourth and fifth cervical levels." I knew I was paralyzed but didn't know why. Or for how long. No one ever explained anything to me about my injury. I'm going to die, I thought. They're just afraid to tell me!"

Little by little I was getting stronger. Eventually Dr. Sherrill scheduled a "fusion surgery." I didn't know all that was involved in fusion surgery but was hopeful it would bring positive results. Following surgery, I was elated to leave the ICU ward and be wheeled into a regular room. It's a sign I'm getting better, I thought. If I wasn't, they'd keep me in ICU. Dr. Sherrill came by. "Everything went fine," he said. "The surgery was a complete success." There was a collective sigh of relief. "Now I want you all to concentrate on the next steps of recovery. There is much progress to be made yet. There will be difficult days ahead, Joni. I want you to know it and brace yourself for them. The toughest part of the battle is the psychological aspect. You're fine now. You've been angry, frustrated, afraid. However, you haven't really been depressed. But wait until your friends go off to college. Wait until the novelty of all this wears off. Wait until your friends get other interests and stop coming. Are you ready for that, Joni? If not, better get ready. Because it'll come. Believe me, it'll come."

"I should have been happy, the surgery was successful, I was getting better, and I was now in my own room. But I wasn't happy. Grief, remorse, and depression swept over me like a thick, choking blanket. For the first time since the accident, I wished and prayed I might die. In this time of depression and questioning, my search led me back to the Bible. I began to sense that God was real and that He was dealing with me. "My thoughts are not your thoughts. My ways are not your ways," He reminded me from His Word. I needed to understand this—that I could not comprehend my own purpose or meaning without taking God's deity into consideration. I did not understand what God was trying to show me, so I prayed: "Lord, I know now that You have something planned for my life. But I need help understanding Your will. I need help in knowing Your Word. Please, God, do something in my life to help me serve You and know Your Word."

"It was summer, 1969, two years after my diving accident. I thought of the many things that had happened to me during those two incredible years. In taking inventory of my spiritual life, I found it consisted mainly of fantastic highs and lows—but mostly lows. Alone with God, I recalled how I'd withdrawn from reality and turned my back on Him so often. I confessed, "Lord, I've been wrong—wrong to try and shut You out. Forgive me, God. Thank You for this new understanding of Your Word. Please forgive me and bring me back to You—back into fellowship with You once more." The Holy Spirit began to convict, then teach me. With each succeeding week, spiritual truth became more real, and I began to see life from God's perspective."

"By February, 1970, I thought, why am I paralyzed? Why is someone else alive and healthy? There was no reason apart from the overall purposes of God. **We aren't always responsible for the circumstances in which we find ourselves. However, we are responsible for the way we respond to them.** I really began to see suffering in a new light—not as trials to avoid, but as opportunities to "grab," because God gives so much of His love, grace, and goodness to those who do. My life changed more during the last half of 1972 than any other period of my life—even my previous five years in the chair. During the fall of 1972, I began to ask serious questions about my future. "Lord," I asked, "What do You have for me?"[1]

The Lord answered that plea in miraculous ways! As each year unfolded, so did the ministry and impact of Joni's life. Joining her in that mission was an amazing high school history teacher who swept her off her feet, so to speak. In 1982, she married Ken Tada who has been by her side ever since, sharing in the ministry of this world-wide endeavor.

What an awesome God we have and how incredible God has been to open the floodgates of opportunity ministering to the disabled people far and beyond what Joni could have ever imagined on that tragic day of her diving accident. Since 1979, the ministry of **Joni and Friends** has touched the world with: "Wheels for the World," retreats and getaways for families with disabilities, international

---

[1] Joni; An Unforgettable Story, by Joni Eareckson Tada and Joe Musser, 1976, 1996, 2001, Zondervan, Grand Rapids, MI.

family retreats, "Cause 4 Life" Internships, Christian Institute on Disability, The Luke 14 Project, and "Joni's House" (outreach centers around the world), just to name a few. In over 50 years in her wheelchair, she has authored books, produced beautiful art, made movies, talks on the radio, produces videos, produced a TV series, speaks to audiences large and small (mostly large) and is periodically featured on the *Joni and Friends* Podcast. For more information please go to www.joniandfriends.org .

When I finally met Joni for the first time, she was in the middle of the church aisle in her super-duper wheel chair motoring towards me. I was one of the choir members participating in the annual Christmas concert which Joni enjoyed and purposed to attend each year. Pacing before the concert began, I headed in her direction to greet her and introduce myself. At the same time, one of the seminary students trotted over to get a photo with her. It was at that moment I realized I was about to meet that young woman on the poster, drawing with a pen in her mouth. I had heard her voice on the radio and seen her many books at the store but for the first time I saw in person her frail and paralyzed body. Even so, her smile and sweet spirit ministered to my soul!

Since meeting her at that festive Christmas concert, I've been fortunate to see her a few more times since my daughter, Crystal, joined the staff of **Joni and Friends.** My favorite time with Joni was at her headquarters in Agoura Hills, CA. My daughter had taken me into her office to say "hi." In our short visit, Joni made the connection that I was one of those choir members at church. Joni then invited me to sing a song with her, she singing the harmony and I the melody. She chose an old Irish hymn which seemed most fitting to capture her heart for the Lord and her calling to reach the world with the truth and love of Jesus Christ:

*Be Thou My Vision, O Lord of my heart;*
*naught be all else to me, save that thou art—*
*thou my best thought by day or by night,*
*waking or sleeping, they presence my light.*

*Be thou my wisdom and thou my true word;*
*I ever with thee and thou with me, Lord;*
*thou my great Father, I thy true son;*
*thou in me dwelling, and I with thee one.*

*Be thou my battle shield, sword for my fight;*
*be thou my dignity, thou my delight,*
*thou my soul's shelter, thou my high tow'r:*
*raise thou me heav'n-ward, O Pow'r of my pow'r.*

*Riches I heed not, nor man's empty praise,*
*thou mine inheritance, now and always:*
*thou and thou only, first in my heart,*
*High King of heaven, my treasure thou art.*

*High King of heaven, my victory won,*
*may I reach heaven's joys, O bright heav'n's Sun!*
*Heart of my own heart, whatever befall,*
*still be my vision, O Ruler of all.*[2]

"Heart of my own heart, whatever befall"…may this be our vision until the Lord calls us home or until the rapture of His church.

---

[2] Be Thou My Vision, versified by Eleanor H. Hull; hymn translated by Mary Byrne

*"Hear my prayer, O Lord! And let my cry for help come to You. Do not hide Your face from me in the day of my distress; incline Your ear to me; In the day when I call answer me quickly. For my days have been consumed in smoke, And my bones have been scorched like a hearth...My enemies have reproached me all day long..."*

*Psalm 102:1-3, 8*

# Chapter

# 7

# The River House

---

*"For momentary, light affliction is producing for us an eternal weight of glory far and beyond all comparison, while we look not at the things which are seen, but at the things which are not seen; for the things which are seen are temporal, but the things which are not seen are eternal."*

*2 Corinthians 4:17-18*

In the summer of 1987, while pregnant with her third child, Janell took a trip to San Diego to visit her grandmother. The revelation which occurred while there would change her perspective for future events to come. At that time, her husband had been struggling with Hodgkin Lymphoma and was going through a series of radiation treatments. She struggled with the thought of losing her husband even though she knew he would be welcomed in heaven. Her thoughts of being a single parent and raising three kids on her own brought her to tears. Could she handle this task? She was challenged by the thought, "Do you believe the Lord? Do you trust in God? Yes or no?" Her answer was YES! This became the turning point for her, realizing and trusting that the Lord God Almighty could take care of her, her family and her future.

Returning to her home in Oregon, Janell gave birth to a healthy baby boy, Jason. Life continued to look hopeful as her husband, Joel, improved and continued to serve as the pastor of Faith Baptist Church. As a full time mother, Janell was faithful to keep her reliance and trust in the Lord. Their three children continued to grow into mature godly adults who walked alongside Janell, not realizing that Joel would later contract Mesothelioma, a cancer as a result of the radiation. However, it wasn't until 2011, twenty-four years later, that Joel would be called home to be with the Lord. Who would have thought the Lord would give Janell twenty-four more years with Joel after that encounter in San Diego.

I've always thought Janell to be laid back, systematic and logical but I didn't realize how foundational the Lord was in developing her character. When I saw her last year for a reunion of college students from the University of Arizona, she seemed wiser but also confident in her new endeavors which included buying and renovating a couple of homes. As I viewed the progress of one of her houses being renovated in Oregon along a beautiful river, I was captivated and amazed by her stamina and determination to make that River House as beautiful as its surroundings. Needless to say, son Jason and daughter Jodi pitched in to assist in this project which continued to unfold and broaden. First, the renovation of the master bath was accomplished...then refreshing the living room, vaulting the ceiling, adding dormers, stripping and redoing the flooring, retiling the kitchen floor, removing the fireplace and adding a bedroom. With eldest son, Jesse, advising from Montana via phone, the improvements to the house seemed endless. On and on it went until a stunning, updated, fresh and open River House was ready to inhabit and rent through www.airbnb.com.

By June the beautiful River House was rented for short-term periods. In September some young businessmen, wanting to work remotely, rented the house presumably to get out of the COVID craziness. Labor Day weekend looked to be a beautiful time to spend in Oregon along the McKenzie River. That is, until Janell received a call from the renters late that Labor Day evening complaining that the electricity had gone out. Janell advised them of the location of the candles. She also knew the water pump was electric which could add to their discomfort. Little did the men know that six miles from the house the Holiday Farm Fire was heading their way. Later that evening, one of the men at the house saw flames of fire through the windows. He quickly roused the others, grabbing what they could, and headed out of the area. The wind was whipping. Ashes were swirling. Trees were crashing to the forest floor. Emergency vehicles came rushing in as smoke was enveloping the entire area. Fortunately the men were able to get out in time to find safety, thirty-five miles away to a hotel.

For Janell, she could only pray and wait for authorities to release public information regarding the damage of this fire. Facebook messages plus phone calls were sent out for prayer while Janell reminded the Lord of all the work she had done to make this house so spectacular. God wouldn't let it burn down, would He? Waiting day after day seemed like an eternity. After one week had passed, a sheriff friend was able to get into the area to check on the house by the lot number. Photos were taken. The news was conclusive. The River House had turned to ashes. Scorched trees and blackened stumps dotted the once-lush forest. Everything seemed lost in the fire, including a large one hundred-year-old family photo that hung on the wall of the living room.

This active fire grew to 145,000 acres, one of at least ten wild-land blazes that threatened communities all across Oregon. It would be a total of three weeks since the Holiday Farm Fire was at its peak, before Janell would be able to go into the area to see what remained in the ashes of the River House. Fortunately, Jason accompanied her to the location to stir through the charred remains. Because all of her hiking boots burned in the fire, she borrowed a pair from Jason which gave her "some big shoes to fill." To break up the sadness of the day, she and Jason thought to bring their fishing poles to see what was biting. Whether they caught anything or not, it was just good to be near the river remembering many other good times together.

Returning to her home base in Albany, Janell reviewed the to-do list now in front of her. What was the first thing to accomplish? It was to have that conversation with the Lord. Would she trust Him to handle the details of this tragedy, to rely on His comfort, His wisdom, His peace? Looking into God's Word, His promises made so long ago still seemed relevant for her at this time. Jesus reminds us, "These things I have spoken to you, so that in Me you may have peace. In the world you have tribulation, but take courage; I have overcome the world." (John 16:33) Janell has chosen to rest in God's peace. She knows life is full of challenges. She realizes that she doesn't have to understand all that is going on in the world or in her life, but she does choose to walk through this fiery trial knowing Jesus Christ has the best plan for her. Yes or No? Do you believe? Do you trust Him with your whole heart? In Him we can take shelter. In Him we can be assured of His comfort, and an ever-present help in time of trouble.

*When you pass through the waters, I will be with you; And through the rivers, they will not overflow you. When you walk through the fire, you will not be scorched, nor will the flame burn you. For I am the Lord your God, The Holy One of Israel, your Savior.*

*Isaiah 43:2-3*

*"Sometimes God doesn't deliver us from the fiery trials we face. Instead, He delivers us through them. When He does, we experience His love through His presence....The God who loves you is also able to save you from the fire you face, though His love may choose not to prevent your fire. Even so, His love will be present there. Sometimes we see God's love for us most clearly when He chooses to endure the sorrow with us, to feel the pain right there beside us."*
*Jennifer Rothschild*

*"Now may the God of **hope** fill you with all joy and peace in believing, so that you will abound in hope by the power of the Holy Spirit."*

*Romans 15:13*

# Chapter

# 8

# Nancy's Story

---

*"The Lord is my shepherd, ... He restores my soul;*
*He guides me in the paths of righteousness for His name's*
*sake. Even though I walk through the valley of the shadow*
*of death, I fear no evil, for You are with me; Your rod*
*and Your staff, they comfort me."*

*Psalm 23:1-4*

Overlooking a beautiful lake in southern California, I was inspired to finish writing my third book. While in that area, I would often attend a small church on each Sunday. After meeting some of the people from this church, one sweet lady encouraged me to meet a woman named Nancy, thinking we had a lot in common. We were both Christians, both conservative and we were both passionate about letting our light shine in the culture in which we lived, locally and nationally. Ironically…we were both blonde.

It wasn't until several months later when I was traveling and speaking in southern California that I would visit this small church again. Oddly enough I was talking with another woman, who thought I should meet…yes, you guessed it, the one and only Nancy Sandoval. This was the same woman the other lady wanted me to meet. It was on that Sunday after church I finally met Nancy.

We became great friends and have had many convivial times together along with her husband, Paul, and her very large family of seven children and fifteen grandchildren. There was a period of time I also lived with them in their five bedroom house. I often made my own dinner which usually consisted of a salad and some kind of protein. They would often tease me about the salads, thinking that was all I ever ate. One evening while making my dinner salad, I tossed some chopped broccoli in my mouth. Instantly realizing the broccoli had lodged in my throat, blocking my airway. I knew I was choking but Nancy and Paul were upstairs with no clue that I was fading fast. So I floundered up the stairs to find Paul and Nancy, trying to communicate to them that I was choking. Nancy yelled for Paul to give me the Heimlich. After several tries, the broccoli finally cleared my passageway so that I could breath once again. Paul literally saved my life!

It would be a couple years later that I would convey this event to Paul's family and friends...at his memorial service. Paul had developed some lung issues, namely Pulmonary Fibrosis (the scarring of the lung tissue). They gave him three to five years to live. The doctors also found a cyst on the head of his pancreas. It was suggested that Paul have a Whipple operation to remove this cyst while he was still healthy and lungs were clear. On Thanksgiving 2019, the family agreed and Paul decided to get the operation completed so he could enjoy being home for Christmas.

The surgery was scheduled for December 4th. All went well, so they thought. The cyst was removed but Paul was not recovering as they all hoped and prayed. Eleven dreadfully awful, lamentable days later, Paul went home to be with the Lord. Nancy and the family were shocked and heartbroken. Exhausted and stunned, Nancy left the hospital to go home to an empty house and a Christmas tree erected pre-surgery by Paul, bare of any decorations. Fortunately, one daughter from Denver had flown in just in time to say her "good-bye" to her father and would stay at the home with Nancy.

With the holidays upon them, Nancy cried out to the Lord for help, for peace, for guidance, for something that would help her understand God's plan in all this grief. Her mind became preoccupied with the upcoming events of Christmas, New Years, then in January, Paul's birthday and her own birthday. Because she was the queen of organizing and gathering her family together, she felt there was barely any time to grieve. Even though her depression weighed heavily, she felt the Lord urging her to lift up her head, go to church and stop sulking in her home. Sunday came and when arriving at church she felt safe to sit next to another woman who seemed preoccupied and very unhappy. As it turned out, this woman had lost her husband just two weeks prior and was grieving as well. Nancy knew the Lord would use her somehow to minister to this woman, supporting her with a listening ear. As time passed they became good friends and shared many meals and times together.

Strangely coincidental, a neighbor just four houses up the street relayed her sympathy to Nancy, mentioning that she too had lost her husband seven days before Nancy lost Paul. The Lord assured Nancy that He would minister to these new widows through her life, coming alongside them knowing exactly how they were feeling. Nancy pondered what to say and was convinced they just needed to know that someone cared. She realized when others would say positive things about Paul (like, "he was such a nice guy"), she would feel more sadness and miss him more than ever. She, too, needed others to come alongside her just to show they cared without explanation.

In the meantime, there was the need of organizing Paul's memorial. With COVID restrictions beginning to close in on gatherings, rapid planning seemed necessary. It wasn't until mid March, Friday the 13th, that the memorial was scheduled. Friends and family crowded into the large tent-church to celebrate Paul's life and to comfort those experiencing this unexpected loss. After the dust settled from such a memorable event, Nancy could finally let down and be totally enveloped in her grief.

With mandates from our State's Governor, staying sequestered at home because of a virus was NOT what Nancy wanted or needed. She began to sink into deeper depression, only to be encouraged by reading a book called <u>When Jesus Speaks to a Hurting Heart</u> which paraphrased God's Word. She explained that she "couldn't handle complicated" so reading the simple passages aided in comforting her troubled soul as in the following message: "On your darkest day, in your deepest crisis, when you cannot take one more step, I am near. I will take hold of you, I **will** rescue you!"[3] From Psalm 18:16 NIV she read, "He reached down from on high and took hold of me; He drew me out of the deep waters."

Many of her days were spent lamenting on her favorite family-room couch. She couldn't wait until evening, knowing she could go to sleep soon and be done with the night. In the morning, she dreaded having to get up to go through another depressing day. Then she would be reminded that "You have never cried a tear that I did not see. You are My precious one. I loved you enough to die for you. I am right here, even on the saddest day of your life."[4] "You keep track of all my sorrows. You have collected all my tears in your bottle. You have recorded each one in your book." (Psalms 56:8 NLT) Reading through the book of Psalms was one of the few things that would help to gain perspective and bring comfort to her soul.

---

[3] Emily Biggers, <u>When Jesus Speaks to a Hurting Heart</u>, (Uhrichsville, Ohio, Barbour Publishing, Inc.) 2015

[4] Ibid.

By God's grace, her doctor gave her medication which helped bring chemical balance back to her depleted body. Nancy had not only gone through these months of grief but came down with the coronavirus which progressed into pneumonia. She lost weight and lost her sense of taste so food was not even appealing. She would be reminded, "Do not let your heart be troubled; Believe in God, believe also in Me." (John 14:1) Then she would read, "I know you are afraid. Allow Me to replace fear with assurance and anxiety with peace. Ask Me to increase your faith, and I will. I stand ready to rescue and ready to comfort."[5]

She gradually began to feel the Lord pulling her out of a deep, dark hole, setting her on level ground again. The lock-downs were still affecting her ability to get out to be with people. Her creativity kicked into high gear, organizing a "widow gathering" on her driveway in front of her house. Those whom she recently met who had lost their husbands along with some close friends (like me) brought their lawn chairs and beach umbrellas, sharing chips and dip and other hors d'oeuvres. Nancy ministered to them and they in turn encouraged her. Just being together, sharing their stories and their joys was the best medicine of all.

With restrictions still hovering over our cities and state, we heard of a pastor who felt led of the Lord to open his church. His conviction rang true as we were reminded: "…let us consider how to stimulate one another to love and good deeds, *not forsaking our own assembling together,* as is the habit of some, but encouraging one another; and all the more as you see the day approaching." (Hebrews 10:24-25) On May 31, 2020 Calvary

_____

5 Ibid.

Chapel Chino Hills opened…and opened wide!! We were thrilled to attend church once again *in person*!! Nancy was thrilled and would often ride with us to church even though it was a 40 minute drive. What a blessing to sing praises together and hear the Word of God preached while gathered together. Nancy was blessed as she became faithful to attend almost every Sunday.

Along with this blessing was a small group of believers who would gather together mid-week to listen to the pastor and pray for one another. Nancy knew she should **not** isolate herself from those who could love her unconditionally and pray for her week after week. She also realized how important **she** was to the others in the Body of Christ, considering how to stimulate each other to love and to do good deeds. She was learning afresh how to lay down her emptiness and ask to be filled with the Holy Spirit, remembering where the solution to her problems are found, not in the world, but in the Lord Jesus.

*"I love you, O Lord, my strength."*
*The Lord is my rock and my fortress and*
*my deliverer. My God, my rock, in whom I*
*take refuge; My shield and the horn of*
*my salvation, my stronghold.*

*Psalm 18:2*

*"There is nothing that can replace the absence of someone dear to us, and one should not even attempt to do so. One must simply hold out and endure it. At first that sounds very hard, but at the same time it is also a great comfort. For to the extent the emptiness truly remains unfilled one remains connected to the other person through it. It is wrong to say that God fills the emptiness. God in no way fills it but much more leaves it precisely unfilled and thus helps us preserve, even in pain, the authentic relationship."*

*~ Dietrich Bonhoeffer*

# Chapter

# 9

# Loss of Freedom

---

*"After you have suffered for a little while, the God of all grace,
who called you to His eternal glory in Christ, will Himself
perfect, confirm, strengthen and establish you. To
Him be dominion forever and ever. Amen."*

*1 Peter 5:10-11*

In the year of 2020, we found ourselves restricted, masked, isolated and pronounced non-essential because of a virus. As an American with freedom given by our Creator substantiated in our United States Constitution, living through that year was reminiscent of a time in my life when I lived in the Middle East. My freedom there was restricted, at least for an American woman. I felt isolated, held up in our living quarters. The following is an excerpt from my recent book, <u>Living Under Sharia Law; Viewed Through the Veil of an Infidel</u>:

Who could have imagined the challenges awaiting our little family as we packed to travel to a far-away country for a new cultural adventure. My husband had taken a teaching position at King Abdullah Aziz University where he would teach English as a second language. This was his area of expertise, having done so at the University of Arizona and now preparing to do so in Jeddah, Saudi Arabia. He felt led to go to this location because of a desire to bring the Good News into a land that would not allow anyone to do so...to evangelize. This land where Mecca is the epicenter of Islam. This land where there are no Buddhist temples, no Hindu shrines, no Catholic cathedrals, no Mormon tabernacles, no Christian churches and definitely no Jewish synagogues.

We would indeed encounter a new cultural experience. The children would be homeschooled and would most likely pick up another language such as Arabic during our time in this country. We were anticipating the best. So my little family, which included two young daughters, age 22 months and a three year old, obtained passports and began the process of packing for our supposed five-year stay in Saudi Arabia.

Finally, the day came to board our flights across the world, having just gained our visas special delivery that same day. We were ready, we thought, for what the future would hold. We would fly from Arizona to London with the thought of doing some sight seeing as well as beginning our time change acclimation. You know how that jet lag can be! I always feel a bit "upside down" when I travel across the pond, either the Atlantic or Pacific.

After spending a couple days seeing the sights in London, we boarded another plane flying over Europe and Egypt, into Saudi Arabia. When de-boarding the plane, the atmosphere seemed oppressive and dark. The customs workers went through our luggage as if we had hidden some rare gems which they were wanting to confiscate. Clothes were tossed and not returned to its neat and tidy order of packing. Our travel trunks were hijacked unless we paid the extra fees for having too much weight on each of our flights. We were graciously picked up from the airport by another teacher from Britain who also worked in the same department at the University where my husband was hired. It seemed like we drove for hours to arrive in the city of Jeddah where he delivered us to an apartment building. This would be our home provided by the University for the duration of our stay.

As we settled in, putting the children to bed would be my first priority. The flights were long and wearisome. I never anticipated what would occur next. At the moment the children got into bed, it collapsed. Yes, the entire bed frame gave way. If we weren't so tired, we might have laughed at the incident. But at the time, it was more of a shock and not funny at all! So we decided to pull out the frame and let the children sleep on the mattress on the floor. As best as I can recall, our children slept there on the floor for the next several months. Fortunately, the bed for my husband and myself stayed in one piece for which I was very thankful. I was not only exhausted from the trip but, did I mention, was exhausted from being pregnant!

Before much time passed, the morning sun peeked through the windows and the call to morning prayer blared out from a loud speaker at the nearby mosque. Much to my surprise this blaring announcement would occur not only early every morning but four more times during each day of every week of every month. I learned that after the call to prayer, any open stores or places of business were required to close during the duration of the prayer time. This was just the beginning of our new cultural experience.

While living at this apartment, I was reminded of the fact that Saudi television only had one station. This TV station was owned and operated by the government. There is a purposeful attempt to control the narrative of news and information in this country. (Sound familiar?) All of the TV shows were in Arabic. This made learning the language more desirous, yet a challenge. One program we enjoyed viewing in Arabic was a cowboy show called Bonanza! It was quite humorous to hear Hoss and Little Joe speaking Arabic about the adventures at their ranch.

Instead of watching TV, more time was spent reading books to my children which I brought from America. In fact, I brought many educational books and tools to use to teach my children which would be fun and interesting. At that time, there was no internet or world wide web, so no google searching or YouTube videos to watch. I'm actually thankful for the time spent with my children reading books, doing puzzles, making crafts, singing songs, playing games and learning more about the world and the love of Christ Jesus.

Because it was SO hot outside, we would often spend most of the days inside the apartment. Some days after my husband returned from teaching at the University, we would go for a ride in the car to the Cornish (seashore). Did I mention, women were not allowed to drive a car/vehicle? So if my children and I wanted to go anywhere we would have to wait to ride in the car with my husband. We could also walk or take a bus. But if we took the bus, we would have to travel in the back of the bus in a special compartment just for women. All the men would be in the large part of the front of the bus.

In the heat of the summer, which seemed to last for many months, we hoped to find a swimming pool for myself and the children to enjoy. Much to my surprise, there were only a couple of hotels which allowed women to swim on one day and men to swim on alternate days. Oddly enough, a man took our money to enter the pool, a man managed the pool, men cooked and served food/drinks at the pool and there was a man lifeguard! My husband was not allowed to come to the pool with me and our children but there were men everywhere working at the swimming pool!

On the weekends (which were Thursday and Friday), we would often go to the beach since we lived near the Red Sea. If we swam in a public place, I would still be required to stay covered from head to toe. I saw Muslim women go into the Sea with their long beautiful dresses and the hijab on their head. One day we decided to drive down the coast as far as the road would take us where we felt alone and private enough for me to sit on the beach with a swimsuit. (Remember now, I was pregnant and felt like a beached whale in one of those skirted maternity swim suits.) Before long, we began to see "spectators" arriving on their motorcycles or in their cars, viewing the arms and legs of an American woman with her husband and two little children. Those arriving were of course men. When my husband told them to leave, he mentioned that the beach is long so no need to park right next to us! The men had varying excuses and would not leave. So we regretfully packed up and called it a day. So much for a lovely day at the beach on the Red Sea. The frustration of adhering to their laws and regulations began to cramp our lifestyle that we were used to in the United States.

We knew this country was ruled by the King in the heart of Islam under Sharia Law. I just never anticipated the challenge it would be to the freedom we had known living in the United States where "We the People," not the King or the Qur'an, created the guidelines and laws for living. Because of the laws under Sharia, I was required to be covered from head to toe as soon as I left our apartment door to go out in public; legs must be covered down to ankles and arms must be totally covered. Wearing a head covering (hijab) was optional but encouraged. Outside, the weather was already hot! I wasn't at all excited to put on extra clothing just to appease the law, that is, until I found out that I could be arrested and put in jail, if not covered properly.

There were days when I wanted to get out of the apartment to get acquainted with the neighborhood and to let the children experience the culture. One morning we chose to take the bus because it would always get us where we wanted to go more quickly even though the small compartment in the back of the bus just for women was often cramped, smelly, and of course HOT. Nonetheless, I understood that Sharia law did not allow the men and women to mix with one another in social settings such as in a bus.

On one of those days when I had taken the children for an excursion, we became hot and thirsty. So, like most hot and thirsty folks, we found a cafe in which to sit and enjoy some cold juice. Before settling on a vacant table at this patio cafe, two religious leaders proceeded to approach me, beating me with their sticks (much like billy clubs or bobby sticks in England). When I jumped back away from the table to protect my children, a man at another table spoke in English, "It's a MAN's cafe!!" Wow, they could have politely told me that the cafe was for men only but the clerics never seemed the friendly type, especially toward women! So in shock from the experience, I quickly gathered my children and left the cafe. We stayed thirsty until we finally made it back to the apartment with another "not so happy" experience of what life was like living under Sharia law.

When shopping at the Gold Souk, I was interested to find that they sold all pieces of gold jewelry by the gram weight. Most of the jewelry was a high grade of gold, 18-24 karats, and very beautiful. As I found pieces of jewelry I wanted to see or try on, I noticed that as the male clerk would put the piece of jewelry into my hand, he would touch or swipe my hand in a peculiar way. Even as a western woman, the habit of this hand swiping felt very creepy. I found out later that according to Sharia law, a man is forbidden to touch a woman who isn't his wife/daughter/sister. The gold souk clerks were in a sense mocking their laws and using a foreigner to enjoy the inappropriate tactic of touching another woman.

81

No big deal, right? For the gold souk clerks, it's all part of their work ethics with foreign women. Sometimes I would see beautiful jewelry in the shop windows. One time when bending over to look closely at the gems, a man walking behind me put his finger up my rear end. That was a lesson quickly learned and not repeated. My reaction was to turn around and punch the guy who dared to do such a thing. If I had done so, I would have been the one found at fault or arrested for the assault.

Many times when walking back to our apartment, my children and I were followed by men. I would often stop at a store or shop to detour until I felt safe to continue our trek home. When arriving at our apartment building elevator, I would feel uneasy if a man got in the elevator at the same time. So I made it a practice getting out of the elevator, waiting for the next ride up without any men on board. I was rapidly learning the law of the land was not at all friendly to women. That's a nice way of saying their view of women were much like a third or fourth class citizen. Because women are not allowed to hold jobs (except to teach girls or to be a midwife or nurse), men were everywhere in the market place. There were men working at the post office. Men working at the bank. Men working at the grocery store. Men working in the Gold Souk. Men working in the restaurants. I couldn't even buy a dress or undergarment except from a man.

On another day when I was out with my children in the market place, I saw a dress shop with a variety of styles I could wear while pregnant (big and sack-like). While looking at the clothing in the store, a male clerk approached me and wanted me to try on some of the clothes. He took a few dresses for me to try on to the changing room. Once in the changing room, I noticed a mirror overhead which gave visibility for the man at the cash register. I was so infuriated at the thought of him spying on me, I took the pile of dresses back to this man and threw them at his counter and repeated "haram"! (It was one of the few words I had learned and memorized up to this point which is Arabic for *forbidden*.) I gathered my children continuing to shout "haram" until we were out of the store, never to return again!

Wow, it's not like something similar could happen in another country, even the United States. But in our country we could report the incident to the authorities, better business bureau and for sure, Yelp! But in Saudi Arabia the rules are definitely different. In most cases, the woman would be to blame for the crime because she is the cause of "driving a man to do such a thing."

To be assured of more consistent safety, it was recommended that I go out in public with a male escort such as my husband. But as we found through an incident at the Sea, I could not always count on that safety net even with my husband. In fact, when traveling down the highway from a family excursion in the hills of Ta'if near Jeddah, I felt comfortable enough to put my swollen feet up on the car dashboard. (Remember I was pregnant and putting my swollen feet up every now and again was a great relief.) Before long, a car full of Muslim clerics drove up beside our car honking and shouting, shaking their fists, pointing at my feet up on the dash, conveying a message to get my feet down (no doubt because my ankles were showing). Looking at them in amazement, partially wondering what all the fuss was about, my husband finally suggested I put my feet down so we would not get arrested or be driven off the road. I did so. Then the clerics drove off, I assumed satisfied that they made me uphold their laws.

As an American woman, you can imagine my private inner dialogue. "How dare they tell me what to do... and in my own automobile. Who do they think they are, shouting and honking at me. How disrespectful," I thought. But to them, I was breaking another rule/law as laid out in their Qur'an which governs their daily lives and their country. It didn't matter that I was an American citizen or a Christian that didn't believe the same way. To them, I was in their country and I needed to live as their laws and religion dictated.

One evening, when choosing to take a taxi as a family, my husband engaged in a conversation asking the taxi driver many questions in order to practice speaking Arabic. One question arose as to why he did not have a wife yet since he seemed to be of age. The taxi driver replied that he could not afford to buy one yet. Yes, you heard correctly! Women are purchased for wives, some purchased at a very young age, even preadolescent. To buy a wife, we understood arrangements were made through the father of the girl. The man who wished to have a wife would negotiate a price for the girl/woman desired. This taxi driver would someday make a deal with a father of a girl in hopes of buying himself a wife...or two. If he was a wealthy man, he could buy as many wives as he desired.

While teaching in the States, we established a friendship with a Saudi student who attended the University of Arizona. He and his large family lived in Jeddah where we were now living. This student graciously invited us to his family's fortress to meet his parents and all of his brothers and sisters. When visiting and getting acquainted with his family, I quickly made friends with his mother and sisters. We talked openly about customs from both cultures. I wasn't surprised to hear that these young girls/women had dreams and aspirations that were mostly unattainable in their Islamic culture. One girl wanted to be an airplane pilot and another wanted to be a journalist. One of the older sisters had already been given in marriage but pleaded with her father to take her back home because the arranged marriage was very unpleasant for her, to put it mildly. She wished she could choose her own husband someday but that was inconceivable under Sharia law in her Islamic culture.

These teenage Muslim girls told me that when they would go to the shopping areas, the boys would put their phone number on a piece of paper, dropping it in the girl's shopping bag in hopes of receiving a phone call from the girl. The danger, they told me, was when the girl actually phoned the boy so they could talk (in order to get to know each other since dating was not allowed). When and if the girl was caught phoning/talking to the boy, this could be grounds for dishonoring the family, dishonoring the father. A daughter (or wife for that matter) who "dishonors" the father/ family, is encouraged under Sharia law to be killed. Honor killings often occurred as a result under Sharia law, and is not only tolerated but expected.

As time passed, I met some wonderful Filipino nurses/midwives who enthusiastically agreed to help me with the delivery of my baby, that is, until we found out that home births had been recently outlawed. We met these nurses through a series of events when they were in need of a ride to "church." Because there are no church buildings or cathedrals, we found a group of Christians who gathered on a large company compound far, far away from the city center. Within the walls of this compound were street after street of homes clustered around a recreation center with a swimming pool, tennis courts, clubhouse...and yes, a building where we believers met to encourage one another, sing praises and even study the Bible. I thought I had died and gone to heaven! Through this group of believers we met the Filipino women as well as others from India, Africa, Europe, Canada, Britain and the United States.

We were blessed to attend this gathering once a week... until one morning we were met by two Saudi soldiers with machine guns at the entrance gate of this compound. They would not allow us to proceed through the gates. They told us we could not enter and must turn around to leave. What we didn't know at that time was that inside the compound our friends were burying all of the Bibles and hymnals. We were told that if the soldiers found the Bibles, they would be confiscated and burned along with the hymnals that printed praises to our God. We had heard about other situations where a Christian employee might have a Bible at his office work desk. If found, the Bible would be taken and the employee would be deported the next day, no questions asked. It is an understatement when I say I am so thankful for the freedom we have in the United States to worship and exercise our faith in the Lord Jesus Christ...at least for now.

I finally secured a doctor in the seventh month of my pregnancy. He had graduated from Medical school in the United States so I felt confident he could assist me and my husband in delivering our precious baby. In the ninth month, I was ready and anxious to give birth. I looked like a basketball was hidden under my garment. Soon after arriving at the Jeddah Medical Center, our daughter was born healthy and strong! Because there was a cholera epidemic announced in our area, taking the baby out in public was not an option for us. Thus, we were homebound for a few weeks.

One day, when my husband was home from work, I felt confident to entrust the children with him so I could venture out to a nearby neighbor/friend whom we met through the University. It wasn't far, so off I went wearing long pants and long sleeve shirt (much like the Pakistanis wear) but no head covering. I walked with purpose, briskly down the sidewalk making sure I did not look at any man in the eyes or face. After turning the corner next to The Rock Park (a park noted for the large boulders of rocks and very few plants) I heard a shuffling of sandals and then felt a pounce from someone on the rocks above. Down to the ground I went, crushed by the man whose purpose was to rape me. I was so enraged with the assault! When rising up from the pavement in anger, my attacker took off running like a scared rabbit...as if he had seen a ghost. Maybe he did see what seemed to be a ghost...or angels! He took off running at breakneck speed, not looking back for anything...very strange!! At that point I realized that there were angels watching over me. I began giving thanks to the Lord for His protection and care.

I then scurried over to my neighbor where I told them of the incident. They washed my wounds and comforted me. When they asked about the identity of the man, I could only describe his sandals because I was told never to look at a man. Wow, now that is convenient! In a court of law, I not only could not identify my assailant but I would be the one who committed the crime for not wearing a hijab, not to mention the fact that it would be acceptable to rape an infidel.

When I arrived back at our apartment I realized I had enough of living under Sharia law. I did not want to stay in Saudi Arabia for our five-year contract; in fact, I did not want to stay for even one more year, one more month, one more week nor one more day in Saudi Arabia. I resolved to fly back to the United States with my children as soon as our baby could fly without harming her ears. So, the countdown began for me and my three children to secure our flights to go home. One thing we needed was a passport for my new baby and permission from the King to leave Saudi Arabia. My husband would stay an extra six weeks to finish his year of teaching and then he would join us back in the states.

Needless to say, when my children and I returned and arrived in Los Angeles via London, Geneva, and Cairo, I wanted to kiss the soil of these United States of America. I was so thankful to be back in my country of the free and the brave. I was thankful not to be restricted from sitting at a Cafe. I was thankful not to be masked behind the hijab. I was thankful not to be isolated in the back of the bus or to feel non-essential as a Christian woman.

Even now, with all the restrictions that have been placed on us, I am thankful to be an American. The Lord sustained me during my time in the Middle East. He will sustain me through this time of tyrannical control that we've experienced in some of the states of this Republic. My relationship with Jesus Christ has given me peace and hope. Reading and studying the Bible, has given me encouragement and strength for each day. These two things, Jesus and the Bible, are what sustained me through the trials and challenges in the Middle East. Now I am reminded to "Consider it all joy...when you encounter various trials, knowing that the testing of your faith produces endurance. And let endurance have its perfect result, so that you may be perfect and complete, lacking in nothing." (James 1:2-4)

*"So Jesus was saying to those who had believed Him, If you continue in My word, then you are truly disciples of mine; and you will know the truth, and the truth will make you **free**."*

*John 8:31-32*

*Jennifer Rothschild reminds us that, "God may not replace what you have lost, but He will redeem what you have lost. Even your most agonizing loss—even your worst day—will be redeemed as God works it all together for good. Focus today not on the pain of discipline but on the promise of deliverance. Focus not on what you have lost, but on how God is using that loss to grant you greater blessing."[6]*

[6] Jennifer Rothschild, "66 Ways God Loves You" (Thomas Nelson; Harper Collins Christian Publishing, Inc., Nashville, TN.) 2016

# Chapter

# 10

# Loss of Community

*"...for He who promised is faithful; and let us consider how to stimulate one another to love and good deeds, not forsaking our own assembling together, as is the habit of some, but encouraging one another; and all the more as you see the day drawing near."*

*Hebrews 10:23b-25*

When we were asked to *shelter in place* during 2020, many were cooperative for the short duration originally imposed. But when the time was extended, closing businesses, churches and schools, a greater crisis began to implode. The announcement by those in political office stating that some things like businesses and churches were non-essential, stirred up frustration and anger for those fitting into those categories. Why was a local dress boutique non-essential but a large box store *was* essential? Oh that's right, they sold food... but so did the little grocer on the corner down the street from the boutique. As for our public educational system, children were instantly home-schooled, whether their parents were willing or able to take on that task or not. School teachers turned their garages into virtual classrooms to at least see faces and talk with their students about their progress via Zoom. In the meantime, the playgrounds were closed and taped off. Why? Didn't the health advisors know that sunlight is the best disinfectant which would keep the play equipment germ free? Oh wait, the children might show up to play together in the fresh air and sunshine in order to stay strong and healthy. Well-known medical doctors call this togetherness *herd immunity*, which is also a good practice for adults who want to strengthen their immune system.

This concept of "non-essential" should have awakened us from the mesmerizing daily confabulation on most television and cable stations, especially as it relates to the church. How could the community of faith be non-essential? Is it not the body of Christ who serves to help those who are sick and hungry, who are distraught and paralyzed with fear, who need guidance and an understanding word of encouragement? To go through the loss of community was devastating to many, especially those elderly who wanted and needed to see loved ones. If a loved one was captured in a hospital or nursing home, no advocate could come to the rescue. If a loved one passed away during this time, a memorial or funeral was postponed or cancelled all together. For that matter, if your wedding was planned with church and reception, too bad! Being together with family and friends might *endanger* those who might otherwise get the common cold or flu. What happened to taking responsibility for our own health and wellness? Would we not be in greater danger by driving down a busy freeway?

The temptation to hide out in our homes because we feared a virus or we feared death has caused more damage than we anticipated. Was this consequence because God did not design us to be isolated, sequestered in our homes? We were made to be together in a family, in a neighborhood and in a community where we can experience support, encouragement and purpose. Recently I received a brochure from my health provider explaining the fallout of this loss of community. Mental health was the topic. Those who have not been able to see family and friends for a variety of reasons (isolated in elder care, told to stay home to be *safe*, unable to see grandchildren for fear of a virus, etc.) now have or had depression, chronic loneliness, drug overdose and even thoughts of suicide. How sad!

The brochure goes on to elaborate steps to develop a healthy mental outlook, the first point being, yes, you guessed it, *stay social!* Social interaction is one of the most powerful antidotes to anxiety and depression, states the brochure. The next point stated to "lend a helping hand" by utilizing your time and talent even via phone or computer. Because we tend to have a scheduled life, this health provider encouraged taking time to do the things you enjoy on a regular basis. I'm not sure how others were able to accomplish that suggestion when nearly everything was closed or cancelled. But this next point was golden: Take News breaks! It is good to be informed, but a constant stream of news can be very stressful, states the brochure. Better to check for updates just once or twice a day...and from *credible sources*. I love that! How 'bout the credible word of God as one's main source of *good news* to keep mental health intact? This health provider confirms truth found in the Bible, available for consumption every day!

One thing is certain, community **is** essential for every human being, especially those called into the body of Christ. In the body of Christ we are comprised of many different parts: toes, fingers and noses, so to speak. We are not all the same but we all need each other to function as the hands and feet of Jesus to touch the world. We are reminded in the book of Hebrews (10:24-25) to "let us consider how to stimulate one another to love and good deeds, not forsaking our own assembling together, as is the habit of some, but encouraging one another; and all the more as you see the day drawing near."

The Apostle Paul explains how essential the community of faith is in 1 Corinthians 12:14-26: Yes, the body has many different parts, not just one part. If the foot says, "I am not a part of the body because I am not a hand," that does not make it any less part of the body. And if the ear says, "I am not part of the body because I am only an ear and not an eye," would that make it any less a part of the body? Suppose the whole body were an eye—then how would you hear? Or if your whole body were just one big ear, how could you smell anything? But God made our bodies with many parts, and He has put each part just where he wants it. What a strange thing a body would be if it had only one part! Yes, there are many parts, but only one body. The eye can never say to the hand, "I don't need you." The head can't say to the feet, "I don't need you." In fact, some of the parts that seem weakest and least important are really the most necessary. And the parts we regard as less honorable are those we clothe with the greatest care... So God has put the body together in such a way that extra honor and care are given to those parts with less dignity. This makes for harmony among the members, so that all the members care for each other equally. If one part suffers, all the parts suffer with it, and if one part is honored, all the parts are glad. Now all of you together are Christ's body, and each one of you is a separate and necessary part of it. (from Life Application Study Bible)

Wow, the Apostle Paul really nailed it! We all need each other! So during times of closure and isolation, how were we to minister one to another? One major answer to that question lies in the responsibility of pastors/ministers/priests leading their flock to keep the church open and functioning. During the time that churches had been announced as non-essential and were to stay closed, there was one pastor in Los Angeles who preached to an empty church sanctuary leaving the doors unlocked. Week after week, people began to enter the unlocked doors of the sanctuary, hungry to hear the word of God. Before long, the church was full of people who came of their own accord. This pastor knew the importance of Hebrews 10:23b-25. After sending a detailed letter to the California governor explaining the importance and essential nature of the church, not to mention God's authority over the church, this pastor opened the church doors *wide*! When the congregation flooded into the sanctuary, their happiness exploded into a standing ovation for the pastor, an event that never happened before in this conservative Bible believing church.

Another pastor in Chino Hills, California had the same conviction from Hebrews 10:23-25. He prayed and asked the Lord for wisdom. The date, May 31st, came to his mind as the answer to his prayer. Little did he first realize, but that date was Pentecost Sunday. Preparations were made to make sure that all who attended that opening Sunday were sanitized, spaced, and masked (if desired). Thousands came hungry for fellowship and real-live preaching of the word of God. Since that date, many more thousands have come to fellowship in Chino Hills, for some, because the church they once attended was either still closed or not relevant anymore. Other pastors across California and this nation have chosen to obey the Bible, not forsaking the assembling together, encouraging one another in the body of Christ. As a result, the Lord has richly blessed those churches and has opened opportunity for those seeking Truth to join an eternal community as new believers in the Lord Jesus Christ. Life after loss, indeed!

May you be assured of *your* value in the community and may you continually know you are essential to the Lord and the community of faith. "So, as those who have been chosen of God, holy and beloved, put on a heart of compassion, kindness, humility, gentleness and patience, bearing with one another, and forgiving each other, whoever has a complaint against anyone, just as the Lord forgave you, so also should you. Beyond all these things, put on love, which is the perfect bond of unity. Let the peace of Christ rule in your hearts, to which indeed you were called in one body; and be thankful. Let the word of God richly dwell within you, with all wisdom, teaching and admonishing one another with psalms and hymns and spiritual songs, singing with thankfulness in your hearts to God. Whatever you do in word or deed, do all in the name of the Lord Jesus, giving thanks through Him to God the Father." Colossians 3:12-17

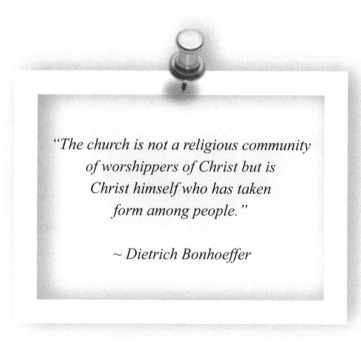

*"The church is not a religious community of worshippers of Christ but is Christ himself who has taken form among people."*

*~ Dietrich Bonhoeffer*

*"The person who's in love with their vision of community will destroy community. But the person who loves the people around them will create community everywhere they go."*

*~ Dietrich Bonhoeffer*

# Chapter

# 11

# Loss of Trust

---

*"Trust in the Lord with all your heart
And do not lean on your own understanding.
In all your ways acknowledge Him,
And He will direct your path"*

*Proverbs 3:5-6*

While trudging through the year of 2020, I found my speaking engagements came to a screeching halt with no conferences, no seminars, no banquets, nowhere to speak. Fortunately, a Texas news outlet recruited me to write monthly articles. This kept me busy researching current events related to the unfolding craziness of that year and beyond. Other journalists with this newspaper were doing the same, exposing truth in hopes of keeping the public well informed. On this journey of writing this book, the Lord brought an incredible patriot to share his wisdom and insight regarding a loss which he is mourning. Join me in viewing this subject through the eyes of retired Colonel Graig L. Carlson. The following reveals his heart and grief for his loss of trust:

"Growing up in a Christian home in the 1950's with WWII-era parents in small town patriotic America was a recipe for inheriting the American Dream. This meant rising to the limits of your abilities in a system that rewarded merit. My brother, sister and I were blessed to be raised by adoring parents without drama in our home. Doors were unlocked at night and rifles were left in gun racks visible to all in the back window of trucks. The streets were safe, people looked out for one another and the police were more like Andy Griffith than Charles Bronson.

My Veteran father was Commandant and Dean of Boys at a Christian academy in Texas. We owned a 300-acre ranch, plus used another 1000 acres leased for raising cows, sheep, goats and three horses. My mother was the glue that held it all together and does so to this day. This was a wonderful time to grow up in America. Television and Hollywood were entering a new age. The programing was positive, patriotic, taught values, and defined what a young person should aspire to be. If you remember the programs "Lassie", "Leave it to Beaver", "Davy Crocket", "Father Knows Best", "Paladin", "Dead or Alive", "Zorro", and "The Lone Ranger" you are fortunate to have lived in that era punctuated by family dinners and church gatherings. I acted out many of my favorite westerns on that little Texas ranch where I learned to shoot straight (in more ways than one) and ride horses. It was an incredibly special time to be alive!

Dwight Eisenhower was the first President I remember hearing and seeing on TV where folks listened with reverence because of a tangible faith in his goodness. People believed in selfless service, honesty, justice, and our government. Church was the center of our social and spiritual world in those days. We were inside the church whenever the doors were open. Extraordinary mentors brought us to a knowledge of the Bible and the many lessons therein.

I remember seeing my first Texas Ranger in a small café in Wimberly, Texas. He was wearing a crisp khaki shirt, matching pants, shined cowboy boots, a gun belt with bullets, and a large revolver on his hip, not to mention a beautiful Stetson. His badge was worn above his left breast pocket and he looked weathered and potentially dangerous to a young kid. The people in the café were captivated by his presence, not for fear but for total respect. When he spoke to my father, I was surprised they seemed to know each other.

My father was not a talkative person but when he spoke you listened because it was usually a life lesson or encouragement. He did not traffic in gossip or condone it. We were raised by our parents to believe anything was possible if we worked to achieve it. We were also taught not to judge people too harshly till you "walked a mile in their moccasins." This meant that all people travel their own road with their own challenges and demons. We did not judge everyone as if they were raised with the same experiences as us or the same affections. We had to learn about demons the hard way as we encountered people away from home that certainly did not have the same values or experiences.

My family believed in public service. My brother and I were raised to understand that we needed to serve our country for a tour of duty in the military, preferably as officers, which meant we would go to college first. Because our parents believed the United States, with all its promise for our peoples' future, it deserved at least two years of our service to educate us about the sacrifice for liberty. As a result, we had a greater appreciation for the life America offered us. It was a natural thing for us to believe, to trust…and we did. My brother served six years and I served 27.

Since then, many things have happened along life's path. The Kennedy assassination was a watershed event that still reeks of sinister musings. It was followed by Vietnam, Martin Luther King, the feminist movement, Madalyn Murray O'Hair, assaults on the family, the abortion horror, 12 presidents of diminished shine, a questionable pandemic, and an unveiling of a propagandist media that has had their undeniable effects. As presidential elections come and go, we seem to choose between the lesser of two evils rather than the most qualified for the job. As a matter of fact, qualifications seem to be a disqualifier in the political realm. I remember meeting Governor John Connally (of Texas) after he had been shot. The public's respect for him stayed unwavering. These were people that held an almost unquestioned trust in our future.

There was no doubt that men like Eisenhower, Kennedy and Texas Rangers were protecting us from evil. These were times that us kids believed in our family and the honesty of a government to protect us. Even when many were building bomb shelters to protect their families in the event of a nuclear attack from Cuba, as kids, we were not deterred from our faith in America and those that were empowered to protect us. That kind of faith in people, government, the media and Hollywood has now faded into a distant memory which is the segue to the topic of this chapter and the loss of trust.

I do not remember the moment movies went from John Wayne's America and good triumphing over evil to movies about how bad the police were or movies denigrating our military. It happened in slow motion along with attacks on our values. Sexuality was front and center. TV shows had male heroes that won the affections of girls in a thirty-minute episode. Women were conquests to be used and disposed. Family values were left in the dust.

My family were Democrats that were left out by the Party during the Lyndon Johnson era and caused them to switch to Republican. The Democrats became the "big tent" party which virtually accommodated anyone that would vote for them regardless of conflicts with traditional values. Religion became an obstacle to their agenda. It still is. Remember the Situation Room program of the 1990s? It allowed government lies to be normalized during the

Clinton administration and was often called the "spin room." It has been an incessant process ever since, undermining real journalism.

The betrayal of our trust became evident. The loss of faith in my own power to achieve our "American dream" began to become a nagging question. As an Army First Lieutenant witnessing the calamity of the Carter years and especially the national embarrassment of "Desert One" (1979 failed rescue mission in Iran) caused me to realize that I needed a closer relationship with God. I became "born again" during those traumatic times and it sustains me to this day. I still claim the prayers of my mother are the only reason I am alive today. The opportunity for things to go wrong in my life have been numerous...sometimes potentially deadly but I have been blessed by prayer. The Army consistently disappointed me with assignments I did not want, but God showed me why I was given those assignments within days of my arrival. Each assignment placed me exactly where God could use the talents He had given me. I had only to be obedient to His plan and His whispered revelations (that most people call conscience).

I encountered wonderful and abhorrent leaders during my service of 27 years in the military. God directed me through the maze of assignments ranging from the foxholes of basic training to the Pentagon and beyond. Discernment and anger management were essential, and neither could have been possible without spiritual guidance. Holding true to my values and standing for what is right never failed to win the day with my superiors and those I led. Trust was a commodity born of faith in God. Even the times that it was necessary to "buck" the system with unwelcome honesty ended up with victory. Sometimes that was a terrible trial that seemed uncertain, but God protected me. There is no other explanation for my successes. I attribute this to my upbringing, faith, and prayer.

My personal failures, and there have been a few, have not been as traumatic as they could or possibly should have been. I learned from those and, for the most part, believe those lessons educated me about the human dimension we navigate through life. My views of the personal failures of others, some far greater than mine, are tempered by those experiences. It allows me to be empathetic which is necessary in this life. Evil is defined as the absence of empathy. We must be able to forgive others and ourselves so the baggage we carry does not prevent us from serving God as we should. If God could love King David, with all his failings, He can love me and you.

Having said all this, the deaths of innocent people in lockdown, nursing homes, suicides, business closures, and poverty brought upon all of us in 2020 may be overshadowed in the long run by the *loss of trust in the systems* of government we were all trusting a mere 30 years ago. President George H. W. Bush ushered in the New World Order and with it, the trust in our governance has been broken. The truth of the corruption and its agenda has been revealed during this "plandemic." From LBJ to Obama, America has been broken in a slow-motion downward sinful spiral. Wars have been fought with no intention of winning. America's youth have been sacrificed for less than protecting our liberty and freedom. We have spent our blood and treasure to please a Satanic greedy force beyond our ability to comprehend. The evil behind this is far worse than we can imagine. It is Biblical.

I see the prophesies being played out before our very eyes and it amazes me that people cannot or will not remove the scales from their eyes to see the truth. We are not the masters of our fate, God is. When many academics deny God as the architect of intelligent design, I have to ask how something as simple as the knee, ankle, eyesight, or reproduction was an accident? Science fails to explain how this "big bang" theory resulted in a planet with oxygen, photosynthesis, water, atmosphere, proper distance from the Sun, and over 1.7 million species is possible. Personally, I do not understand how any observer of nature could possibly deny the existence of God. How do you explain the compassionate tears formed from witnessing an act of love or tragedy? Think of the complicated process of forming that tear and still they deny the existence of God.

Our nation must turn back to God because our battle is against dark forces as defined in Ephesians 6:12: *"For our struggle is not against flesh and blood, but against the rulers, against the powers, against the world forces of this darkness, against the spiritual forces of wickedness in the heavenly places."* God is the answer! We have been deceived for decades by those without morals or empathy. The media has showered us with porn, lust, and mayhem. It is no wonder our society is more dangerous, callous, and self-centered than any time since the fall of Rome. God can and will deliver us from this evil and we will win in the end as the Bible prophesied. We must focus on raising our kids and grandkids with wisdom, values and faith. Pray for deliverance but be prepared to die in service of God's kingdom when called. **Do not shrink from the battle ahead because it is already won.** This is an opportunity to have **revival** in America. Never lose your faith in God. Now is the time to pray without ceasing. Prepare for battle with the full armor of God. And know it is truly an exciting time to be alive!"

Special thanks to Colonel (Retired) Craig Carlson, U.S. Army, Distinguished Service Medal (DSM), Papal Knight (KSG), author of <u>Silent Knight</u>, syndicated columnist, husband and grandfather.

*"It is better to take refuge in the Lord than to trust in man. It is better to take refuge in the Lord than to trust in Princes."*

*Psalm 118:8-9*

*"The great masquerade of evil has played
havoc with all our ethical concepts.
For evil to appear disguised as light,
charity, historical necessity or social justice
is quite bewildering to anyone brought
up on our traditional ethical concepts,
while for the Christian who bases his
life on the Bible, it merely confirms
the fundamental wickedness of evil."*

*~ Dietrich Bonhoeffer*

# Chapter

# 12

# Hope is Here

---

*"Therefore having been justified by faith, we have peace with God through our Lord Jesus Christ, through whom also we have obtained our introduction by faith into this grace in which we stand and we exult in **hope** of the glory of God."*

*Romans 5:1-2*

"Where now is my hope? And who regards my hope?" (Job 17:15) Are we just like Job lamenting those questions? Do you find yourself in a personal argument, going back and forth, trying to talk yourself into some common sense just like Job saying, "Though He slay me, I will hope in Him. Nevertheless I will argue my ways before Him!" (Job 13:15) I love how the Psalmist lays open his heart and affirms, "For I hope in You, O Lord; You *will* answer, O Lord my God...For You are my hope, O Lord God, You are my confidence from my youth." (Psalm 71:5; 38:15)

So where is our hope in times of loss or anytime for that matter? It is *here*, in the presence of the almighty God! In his classic work, Studies in the Sermon on the Mount, Dr. Martyn Lloyd-Jones offers a practical and encouraging perspective for the believer: "Our Lord does not promise to change life for us; He does not promise to remove difficulties and trials and problems and tribulations; He does not say that He is going to cut out all the thorns and leave the roses with their beautiful perfume. No, He faces life realistically, and tells us that these are things to which the flesh is heir, and which are bound to come. But He assures us that we can so *know Him* that, whatever happens, we need never be frightened, we need never be alarmed."

If you are asking, "How can we *know* Him? How can we be assured that our hope is here, in the presence of the God who created heaven and earth, who knows the number of hairs on your head?" There is one reality we can know to be true. It is found in the Bible, the word of God. Truth permeates every page and does not return void. When the Lord Jesus tells us to "fear not" we can be assured that "He's got this!" Remember Janell's story of the

River House and how it burned to the ground after all her work to renovate that property? She chose to trust God, knowing that "God causes all things to work together for good to those who love God, to those who are called according to His purpose." (Romans 8:28)

If you are not sure about your relationship with the Lord, not sure if you have ever really trusted Him with your whole heart, your whole self, then now is the time to give your life to Jesus Christ. He is here, ready to give you hope, ready to give you life, not just here on Earth but forever and ever with Him in Heaven. The Bible tells us, "But as many as received Him (Jesus), to them He gave the right to become children of God, even to those who believe in His name." (John 1:12) Jesus told Nicodemus that even though he was a religious man, he needed to be born again; born of the Spirit. Jesus reminded him, "...that whoever believes will in Him have eternal life. For God so loved the world, that He gave His only begotten Son, that whoever believes in Him shall not perish, but have eternal life. For God did not send the Son into the world to judge the world, but that the world might be saved through Him." (John 3:15-17)

Why do I need to be "saved", you may ask? Saint Paul tells us in his letter to the Romans, "For the wages of sin is death, but the free gift of God is eternal life in Christ Jesus our Lord." (Romans 6:23) Because of our sin (missing the mark of flawless holiness) we cannot have that close, intimate relationship with a perfectly Holy God. But "He (God) made Him (Jesus) who knew no sin to be sin on our behalf, so that we might become the righteousness of God in Him (Christ Jesus)." (2 Corinthians 5:21)

It's not by works of righteousness that we have done but according to His mercy He saves us. Isn't that great news? His love and His saving grace is not dependent on our performance but rather in trusting Him with our whole self. "Blessed be the God and Father of our Lord Jesus Christ, who according to His great mercy has caused us to be born again to a living hope through the resurrection of Jesus Christ from the dead, to obtain an inheritance which is imperishable and undefiled and will not fade away, reserved in Heaven for **you**, who are protected by the power of God through faith for a salvation ready to be revealed in the last time." (1 Peter 1:3-5)

When I was growing up in a wonderful Christian home, I always believed in God. My parents, who met while singing together in a Gospel quartet, loved the Lord and often taught Bible studies in our home and at church. So, when I was asked to take a class at church to become a "member" I didn't think much of it. When we finished the class we were told we could be baptized. I remember being in the baptismal tank and asked if I believed in Jesus Christ, God's Son and Savior. I said yes but thought to myself, "Yeah, doesn't everybody?" I didn't realize that many of those on Earth had not yet heard of Christ.

It wasn't until my sophomore year of high school, when my father took over the high school Sunday class, that I began to understand more fully the teachings from the book of John. My father would teach verse by verse. When we got to John 3, I remember thinking about that "born again" theme with Nicodemus. Shortly thereafter one evening in my own bedroom, I gave my life to Christ asking Him to take over my life, to be my Lord and Savior. The next morning my radio alarm came on and a woman with a folk song voice began singing Amazing Grace! I was stunned to hear this song on the radio station yet assured that God saved "a wretch like me." Throughout the summer months my life and perspective turned around. I remember having a love for myself and a love for others that I never had before. I remember having a confidence and boldness for Christ that I never had before. When I returned to high school that fall of my junior year, my friends wanted to know why I was so different, why I was so much more friendly. They wanted to know what got into me! I let them know JESUS got into me! I knew I was truly born again, having peace with God and a hope for tomorrow that continues to this day.

"Therefore, having been justified by faith, we have peace with God through our Lord Jesus Christ, through whom also we have obtained our introduction by faith into this grace in which we stand; and we exult in *hope* of glory of God. And not only this, but we also exult in our tribulation, knowing that tribulation brings about perseverance, and perseverance brings about proven character, and proven character, hope; and *hope* does not disappoint because the love of God has been poured out within our hearts through the Holy Spirit who was given to us." (Romans 5:1-5)

May you, too, know His peace. And may you know His hope that refreshes your soul. May you always be assured there is real Life after Loss! May God bless you as you walk forward in this new and everlasting life!

*"May God in His mercy lead us through these times; but above all, may He lead us to Himself."*

*~ Dietrich Bonhoeffer*

# About the Author

Becca Keating is a powerful, contemporary voice on the frontline of religion, media, and politics. Keating's urgent first-person perspective on faith and policy are ripped from today's headlines and featured on Talk-Radio, TV and Podcasts. Author of six books, Becca speaks with conviction on the God-given value of every person and the tremendous potential each has to impact family, community, country and the world by the power of the Holy Spirit. The subject matter she brings to the table is *urgently relevant*.

Her passion and fervency is evident in all of her books and speaking engagements. Keating's *Impact Your World* series includes Powerful Communication and the Value of Free Speech, Empowering the Constitutional, Conservative Citizen and Empowering Parents to Educate. She informs, stimulates thinking, and encourages an empowering, positive response to boldly impact lives and our culture for Christ. Her travels to other parts of the world add another dimension to her insight and awareness of the volatile times in which we live. She expounds this in her book: Living Under Sharia Law; Viewed through the Veil of an Infidel.

Becca's contagious enthusiasm creates a high demand for her as a talk show guest, keynote speaker and conference lecturer. To request an appearance with Becca Keating as your special talk-show guest or keynote speaker, go to www.beccakeating.net.

# Notes/Resources

*"The messengers of Jesus will be hated to the end of time. They will be blamed for all the division which rend cities and homes. Jesus and his disciples will be condemned on all sides for undermining family life, and for leading the nation astray; they will be called crazy fanatics and disturbers of the peace. The disciples will be sorely tempted to desert their Lord.* **But** *the end is also near, and they must hold on and persevere until it comes. Only he will be blessed who remains loyal to Jesus and His word until the end."*

*~ Dietrich Bonhoeffer*

Made in the USA
Las Vegas, NV
04 September 2022

54669092R00075